The Smoke and Mirrors Game
of Global CSR Reporting

The Smoke and Mirrors Game of Global CSR Reporting

Issues and Fixes

Anil Hira

ANTHEM PRESS

Anthem Press
An imprint of Wimbledon Publishing Company
www.anthempress.com

This edition first published in UK and USA 2023
by ANTHEM PRESS
75–76 Blackfriars Road, London SE1 8HA, UK
or PO Box 9779, London SW19 7ZG, UK
and
244 Madison Ave #116, New York, NY 10016, USA

British Library Cataloguing-in-Publication Data
A catalogue record for this book is available from the British Library.

Library of Congress Cataloging-in-Publication Data
A catalog record for this book has been requested.
2023933027

ISBN-13: 978-1-83998-805-9 (Hbk)
ISBN-10: 1-83998-805-3

ISBN-13: 978-1-83998-806-6 (Pbk)
ISBN-10: 1-83998-806-1

Cover Credit: Photograph of D.C. People with the national flag of the United States
by Jonathan McIntosh/Creative commons

This title is also available as an e-book.

Dedicated to Dr. Andrew S. Wright, business genius and mentor who dedicated his life to saving the environment for future generations.

CONTENTS

List of Figures and Tables   xi

Acknowledgments   xiii

Introduction: Overview of the Book and Theoretical Concepts   1

1. Corporate Social Responsibility: A Good Deed in Name   15
    Introduction   15
    Corporate Motivations for CSR Are Ambiguous as Is the
    Potential for CSR in Governance   19
        No Clear Definition of CSR   19
        No Profit Incentives for CSR   22
        Questionable Benefits through Consumer Responses   24
        CSR Isomorphism as a Cultural Phenomenon   25
        Institutional Pressures: Unrealized Potential   26
        Conclusion   26
2. The Shell Game of Global CSR Reporting   29
    Global Reporting as the Solution to the Corporate Collective
    Action Problem   29
        The Collective Action Problem   29
        Regimes as a Solution   30
    Mixed Regimes: How International Organizations and NGOs
    Legitimize Corporate Behavior   32
    Case Studies of Global Reporting Regimes: Lots of Reporting,
    Not Much Accountability   36
        The Global Compact   36
        Global Reporting Initiative   39
        Extractive Industries Transparency Initiative   42
    Conclusion: Global CSR Reporting Is Self-Reporting   49

3. Socially Responsible Investment Reporting: A Lucrative
and Growing Business 51
Introduction 51
Evaluating the SRI Indices: Literature Review 56
Methodology of the SRI Indices: A Review 60
MSCI (KLD) ESG Ratings 61
FTSE4Good Sustainability Index 62
Sustainalytics 63
Vigeo-Ethical Investor Research Service 63
Thomson Reuters Refinitiv 64
Bloomberg 65
Limitations of Ratings Methodologies 65
CalPERS: An Example of an Activist Pension Fund's
Perspective 67
Conclusion 69
4. How Human Rights Violations Are Systematically Downplayed
in SRI Systems 73
Serious Human Rights Issues Should Be Reflected in ESG Ratings 73
Mini Case Studies of Ongoing CSR Issues 74
Pascua Lama 74
Vale Mariana Tailings Dam Disaster 76
Apple/Foxconn Suicides 77
Rana Plaza Factory Collapse 78
Methodology: Tracing How Serious Human Rights Scandals
(Deaths) Are Reported in and Affect Ratings 81
Mining 82
Apparel 84
Electronics 85
Do Controversies Affect ESG Ratings? 86
Companies Named in Repeated Issues Are Mostly Covered
by Newsfeeds, but in an Episodic and Haphazard Fashion 86
Money Managers Get Limited and Obscured Data on
Egregious Allegations through ESG Indices 88
Comparing Refinitiv Findings to MSCI Ratings: More
of the Same 94
Summary of How Deaths Are Reflected in SRI ESG
Reporting Systems 96
5. Conclusion: How to Improve the Ratings System Toward
Harmonization, Transparency, and Accountability 97
What Do CSR and SRI Really Mean? 98
Resolving the Collective Action Problem 102

The Governance Paradox   104
Moving to a System Based on Impacts Rather than Gestures
    Requires Shifting Power   106

References   113

*Appendix A: Allegations of Serious Human Rights Violations Related
to Multinational Companies in Mining, Apparel, and Electronics Sectors*   127
    Mining   127
    Clothing and Footwear   131
    Electronics   132
    Other Allegations Based on Amnesty International Reports   133

Index   135

LIST OF FIGURES AND TABLES

Figures

1.1	Corporate Social Responsibility (CSR) Motivations	27
2.1	Evolutionary Layers of CSR Reporting	31
3.1	SRI Ratings Methodology—A Synthesis	60
5.1	The Governance Paradox	105

Tables

4.1 List of Major Mining Companies: Alleged Violent Incidents by Multiple Primary Reporting Sources — 83

4.2 Multiple Listings of Alleged Labor Violations by Major Apparel and Footwear Brands' Subcontractors from Primary Reporting Sources, 2010–19 — 85

4.3 Multiple Listings of Alleged Labor Violations by Major Electronics Brands from Primary Reporting Sources, 2010–19 — 85

4.4 Refinitiv Reporting on Serious Human Rights Allegations in the Mining Sector and Resulting Category Evaluations — 89

4.5 Refinitiv Scores for the Clothing and Footwear Sector around Serious Human Rights Allegations and Resulting Scores — 93

4.6 Refinitiv Scores for the Electronics Sector around Serious Human Rights Allegations and Category Evaluations — 95

ACKNOWLEDGMENTS

I would like to thank the following colleagues for their helpful comments: Leslie Elliot Armijo; SFU's School for International Studies; Glenn Powers (SFU Business); Pacific Northwest Political Science Association, particularly Leif S. Hoffmann of Lewis-Clark State College; SFU's Department of Political Science, particularly Eline de Rooij, Laurent Dobuzinskis, Aaron Hoffman, and Laurel Weldon; and the SFU Clean Energy Research Group for their feedback and support. I would like to thank Patty Hira for editing help, and SFU librarian Mark Bodnar for help in gaining access and learning how to use both the Refinitiv and Bloomberg databases. Parts of the manuscript were vetted with government and corporate officials who work on CSR and ESG and who supported its principal contentions, but prefer to remain anonymous. Finally, I would like to thank several anonymous peer reviewers elicited by Anthem who helped to significantly improve the manuscript.

Introduction

OVERVIEW OF THE BOOK AND THEORETICAL CONCEPTS

There is one and only one social responsibility of business—to use its resources and engage in activities designed to increase its profits so long as it stays within the rules of the game, which is to say, engages in open and free competition without deception fraud.

—Milton Friedman (1962)

Corporations can "do well by doing good."

—Most commonly used phrase to explain corporate social responsibility

Corporations have been under fire from critics in government, civil society, and academics since at least the 1970s. Much of the initial literature relayed the disproportionate power of corporations to many governments and civil society actors (Vernon 1971; Moran 1978). The reasons for such concerns are clear and well-founded—from environmental disasters such as the British Petroleum Horizon blowout in Louisiana to the 2008 financial meltdown, wiping out mortgages and savings of many households. Our purpose here is not to revisit such arguments or to pass moral judgment. Our focus is, in fact, rather narrowly limited to the quality of the information that corporations use to report on their level of corporate social responsibility (CSR). The idea behind CSR is that a corporation has a responsibility beyond profits, more broadly to society beyond its board, shareholders, and employees.

CSR reporting is reaching new heights, with an ever-expanding set of suggested responsibilities and indicators to reflect renewed efforts by corporations to demonstrate they are good citizens, as we discuss at length in the first chapter. In this book, we focus on Western corporations, acknowledging that does not mean corporations from other areas do not have any responsibility. Western corporations have started to operate in an evolving system of elaborate claims, reporting, and challenges around responsibility in highly charged public debates; this gives us a chance to test out the evolving reporting system and how well it's working. The reporting system is the front lines of CSR and we test out whether corporations are following through on their promises.

Our aim in this book is to inform the general debates around CSR through careful analysis of how well current reporting systems are functioning. More importantly, we posit that CSR reporting systems offer an underestimated potential fulcrum for much-needed social change in a variety of areas, from labor standards to climate change to inequality. As of this writing, the most recent climate change talks in Glasgow were accompanied by a bold pledge by the former Bank of England Governor Mark Carney that the private sector will offer $130 trillion in capital for climate change. The opacity of such a pledge, like countless others, has led to accusations of "greenwashing," counting already made investments and the fact of continuing financial support to the fossil fuel industry (Walker and Hodgson 2021). Corporations will only be incentivized toward greater (nonprofitable) responsibility if they get credit for genuinely transformative (and costly) actions. In turn, incentives for changing corporate behavior only exist if there is a robust and transparent information system, so corporations can get "credit" for their good deeds, and be held accountable for their transgressions in terms of environmental damage and labor standards. Thus, our focus here is on whether there is a robust and reliable information system behind CSR. By testing out the system, we show its many flaws as well as ways forward for improvement, such reform could create a solid foundation for a real-life CSR.

Why CSR? CSR is one of the fastest-growing areas of business activity. Virtually every business school teaches, and every major company has, a CSR strategy. To be more specific, 90% of companies on the S&P 500 index published a CSR report in 2017, up from just 20% in 2011. An estimated 80% of all major global companies have a CSR report, and 96% of the top 250 companies do (KPMG 2017, 2020). The most recent estimate we found was from 2013 when Global Fortune 500 companies were spending $20 billion per year on CSR (Varkey 2016), a figure that surely has increased considerably since then. *The question this book starts with is, how well spent are the $20 billion in annual CSR investments?* Astonishingly, there are no readily available metrics by which to answer this question.

A Harvard Business School Report notes the following statistics that highlight why businesses are investing more effort into CSR (Stobierski 2021):

- 70% of Americans think it's important for companies to make the world a better place; 55% believe that companies should take a stand on major social, environmental, and political issues

- 41% of millennial investors, 27% of Gen X, and 16% of baby boomers state that they consider a company's CSR in making investment decisions
- 93% of employees in the United States state that companies must lead with purpose; 95% state that businesses should benefit all stakeholders, including communities
- 90% of executives believe that a strong sense of collective purpose drives employee satisfaction

CSR, in short, is an inescapable element of strategy for large businesses. There is, consequently, a significant and growing CSR industry of reporting, auditing, aggregating, consulting, and assessing that lacks precise estimates but surely is in the hundreds of millions. Business scholars celebrate a dawn of change in business activities, that such shifts reflect. New business models see the significant role that the private sector can play in offering technological, financial, and management skills to social and environmental problems, even as the businesses see such issues as part of their responsibility as good citizens to solve (Bocken et al. 2014). Harvard professor Michael Porter popularized the notion of compatibility between profits and social responsibility through the term "shared value," stating that companies need to recognize "that societal needs, not just conventional economic needs, define markets." On a broader scale, scholars see that business is starting "to assume social and political responsibilities that go beyond legal requirements and fill the regulatory vacuum in global governance" (Scherer and Palazzo 2011).

There are at least four major reasons given for broadening measurements of corporate performance beyond financial return: appeals to morality and citizenship; the need for sustainability in that environmental conditions or poor education or health care, etc. will affect businesses' ability to operate successfully in the long run; the need for a "social license" to operate, so society can shut down or prevent "bad actors"; and the benefits to corporate reputations and brands, as reflected most clearly in companies that make sustainability part of their brand, such as Patagonia. Regardless of the ultimate source, what is clear is that corporate social responsibility is a factor for shareholders in judging management performance (Yuan et al. 2019), and that it may play a role in attracting and retaining highly qualified employees (Ng et al. 2019). Similarly, CSR corporate governance issues such as increasing diversity are argued to lead to better financial performance as well as social and customer support (Hoobler et al. 2018). CSR is also increasingly seen as a reflection of managers' personal values (Hemingway and Maclagan 2004).

In the business literature and world, this is celebrated as a shift toward the "triple bottom line" of profit, social, and environmental measures of performance. CSR performance should thus be measured alongside financial performance.

In some cases, these could clearly work together, such as improving energy efficiency to reduce energy costs. In many other cases, however, the differing goals of profit and social responsibility do not clearly mesh, and measurement of them is very problematic. We return to this question throughout the book.

Before we get to that we should also acknowledge another side of the debate, as reflected in the general critiques of the sustainability of global capitalism (Jacobs and Mazzucato 2016). Arguably, these date back at least to Polanyi's (1944) discussion of the need to temper capitalism's excesses through social regulation at the turn of the twentieth century. While orthodox Marxism may have seen its best days behind it, more recent variations such as the regulation school continue to point to the inherent contradiction of markets that rely upon institutional rules for their functioning, such as contract enforcement, while at the same time suggesting any interference in markets is suboptimal (Boyer and Saillard 2001). Such critical perspectives are important, for examining the way that our economic systems operate at the global, national, and local levels, and to whom the costs and benefits of the system accrue. Changing the capitalist system would require revolutionary change, and a prerequisite to that would be a breakdown of the system. We do not see the system as anything near collapse. Moreover, for system change to take place, one needs to offer a cogent, convincing, and pragmatic alternative to global capitalism, one that critics have yet to offer. Simply put, critics do not seem to have any clear recommendations for changing policy or for how social movements can spark systemic change. More fundamentally, they ignore the basic paradox of their critique—that power resides primarily with states and corporations, and not with revolutionary forces. Unless there is a major crisis that upends power relations, only states and corporations, responding to civil society pressures, can instill change.

There is no question that corporations are serious power brokers, influencing the course of politics through lobbying, often under the veneer of CSR and "charitable giving" and more direct campaign contributions to their political allies (Bertrand et al. 2020). Yet, for the moment, civil society is not pushing for radical change; people, in general, are not calling for a shift toward government ownership or highly progressive taxation, for example, even as populist movements signal growing unhappiness at forces such as inequality and slipping living standards (Hira 2019). What we are proposing in this book is rather more narrow and *pragmatic* in its approach to provide information that can shift things in the immediate term in a realistic manner. That is, by providing accurate information on the state of CSR reporting so that business managers, policymakers, and more importantly civil society actors, particularly institutional representatives such as pension fund holders and activist shareholders, can be empowered to push for change. The change we are proposing here will not appear to be radical on the surface, but it will be radical if put into practice, akin to the workplace safety and social safety net regulations enacted at the beginning and middle of the twentieth century in Western societies, enabling a middle class to rise. The same protections through CSR can create a global middle class (Hira 2006) and sustainable production in regard to climate change. We focus on reporting as a first step in this transformation; no transparency or accountability for the CSR promises companies or investment fund managers presently make means that such promises are all too often vacuous.

Most of the work in Global Political Economy has underplayed the role of corporations in favor of states. Indeed, we have only nascent theories about companies in stark contrast to the many theories about state action both on the international and domestic levels. The lack of state activity on the global level to manage corporate activity via regimes is breathtaking in its absence; CSR is essentially a reflection of an almost complete lack of global regulation. It's true that states, if they work together, are far more powerful than corporations, as illustrated by the nascent global minimum tax agreement that was being negotiated in 2021. The very general work on varieties of capitalism (Boyer 2005; Hall and Gingerich 2009) signals differences between Anglo-Saxon "liberal" market economies from continental European Union (EU) economics such as Germany and France, which might lead some to differentiate CSR in the two regions. However, these geographic differences are not significant for CSR ratings, which are designed for global, not regional investors, shareholders, and supply chain partners.

Even with expected resistance from other countries' MNCs, the fact is that large Western corporations will have a strong hand in determining the quality of life and sustainability for the planet, thus the West has largely defined what is meant by CSR on the global level. Global CSR regimes reflect the common agreement of both EU-, US- and Canadian-based firms responding to shared pressures by pension holders around socially responsible investment (SRI) even while some ratings firms cater more to EU than US clients and vice versa. Regardless of the geographic propensity of any individual investors or firms about where to list/look for their ratings needs, the mechanisms by which they operate are quite similar. Indeed, most ratings agencies contain a wide mix of both US- and EU-based firms.

The EU in particular has been an important actor in pressuring corporations toward responsibility. In pushing for digital services taxes and greater privacy protection, for example, it has recognized the need for a new regulatory approach to the digital economy. The EU has also set up the European Trading System (ETS), a cap-and-trade approach to reducing carbon, however, by and large, it is an umbrella approach that leaves it up to corporations to decide how to reduce emissions. So far, the ETS is largely viewed as a failure in creating a transition away from fossil fuels. The EU still relies heavily on natural gas and has yet to phase out coal. Similarly, the EU's new approach to sustainability regulations for imports and its proposed carbon border adjustment tax could spur changes in corporate behavior abroad in rather indirect ways. These laudable proposals will fall short if North America and Japan do not follow along, as illustrated in the current efforts around creating a global minimum corporate tax.

Moreover, even the boldest EU proposals offer only an indirect stick of enforcement, and no real "carrot" or positive incentive for improving supply chains. In fact, any global regulation or enforcement will depend on an information system that is currently missing, as described here, and the capacity of the global South to comply is open to question, so incentives to take shortcuts for compliance will abound. More importantly, the EU's forward-looking initiatives will be undermined unless there is harmonization with Canada, Japan, and the United States to create enough global momentum toward establishing regulatory and reporting standards. Absent reporting, compliance with the most aggressive sustainability policies is *not* assured.

The West has the power to push for global CSR standards. As controllers of access to the largest markets in the world other than China, together the Western states have latent unused power, power that can only be wielded for social aims if harmonized and exercised toward CSR. But first, it has to model such behavior, by enacting meaningful CSR; only by "walking the walk" can such norms and principles become global.

Another problem with CSR relates to what types of norms are to be adopted. Whether and how much global regulation of companies occurs is a major node of contention, reflecting the common challenges of any social reform—too many fragmented actors working in different currents, from activist shareholders to NGOs to international organizations. Nonetheless, the overall push for reform is palpable, including the increasing recognition of labor conditions, as reflected in the contention around Qatar's hosting of the 2022 World Cup, and even more so in recognition of the environmental costs of production, most prominently climate change, but including biodiversity, rainforest loss, sea-level rise, and a host of other related issues. There are equally weighty concerns about growing inequality in the West. Such concerns spill over into tax evasion and CEO pay. Social movements championing reform will undoubtedly continue to play a major role in raising awareness and political pressure on government and corporations to address such issues. Initial movement responses include anti-globalization populism.

However, such movements are unlikely to succeed in the long run because much of globalization is already irreversible, with supply chains and markets for a wide range of products spanning the globe (Hira 2019). The reality of globalization was brought to the forefront in 2020 with the global COVID-19 pandemic which revealed all of the challenges of a fragmented, domestically based set of policies and regulations to respond to global-level crises. This reinforced the sense of concern from the 2008 financial crash which revealed the intertwined nature of global finance; the fragility and complexity of financial agreements; and the challenges for domestic governments to improve regulations (Hira, Gaillard and Cohn 2019). Such concerns have led to thus far haphazard attempts to enforce Western domestic standards on corporate activities abroad (Rioux and Vaillancourt 2020). While genuinely motivated, CSR so far lacks a system of regulation, including reporting.

In examining how to start to build such a system, we do not seek to create a new academic theory, instead, we seek to reach a wider audience to include policymakers, business and investment managers, and activist shareholders, and our primary aim is to motivate actionable reform. Nonetheless, it's worth noting the importance of academic theories and concepts underlying this work. One particularly important concept is that of "externality" from economics. Externalities are costs or benefits not borne by the producer or consumer (Pigou 1920). The classic example is pollution, which when borne into common air or waterways will affect the general population, not just those who come in contact with it. A related concept is that of "discount rate," where costs borne in the future are underestimated by current market participants; climate change is a classic example where rationality fails because of myopic understanding of discount rates. Thus, we have at least two clear market failures that affect sustainability—externalities and irrational discount rates that ignore long-term costs.

There are two possible solutions to externalities issues. One is to internalize them. An example of this would be the idea of "extended producer responsibility," so that a manufacturer would be responsible for the disposal of waste products and emissions as well as the product itself. The other way is to use regulation, which can take on a very wide array of forms, from bans (such as those on harmful CFC production) to requiring lower emission standards to providing subsidies for new technologies to change production systems through carbon taxes or to "internalize" the external costs through tradable permits (Pigou 1920; Coase 1960). Another prominent suggestion is to create a cap on externalities and then allow trading for the right to pollute. One would slowly lower the cap over time, thus incentivizing innovation in pollution-reducing devices by the private sector. Regardless, there is clearly a place for regulation where markets fail (Jaffe et al. 2005).

The current CSR system assumes that there are positive externalities for good corporate behavior, but externalities by definition do not sufficiently motivate behavior. The challenge is how to create regulation around global activities given clear market failures.

A second important concept that we draw upon from economics is the idea of "transactions costs." These are frictional costs that prevent a buyer or seller from smoothly making a deal. They could involve anything from distance between the two, requiring transport of the product, to differences in access to information, such as the oft-used example of buying a used car. An equally important concept is the "principal-agent" problem, whereby a purchaser of a service, such as a home purchaser, enlists the help of an expert, such as a real estate agent, to work out contract details. In both the used car and home purchase examples, the key problem is "information asymmetry," a problem discussed much in the economics literature (Akerlof 1970; Stiglitz and Rothschild 1976). Without clear information, markets can break down or create lopsided deals in favor of the person who knows more. In the case of CSR, corporations naturally control almost all of the information about what they are doing. Thus, CSR reporting, which is largely self-reporting, suffers from a conflict of interest and creates a "transactional power" that is lopsidedly in favor of the corporation. A prime example is widespread concerns about global tax evasion as reflected in news stories around the Panama and Paradise papers (Hira et al. 2019).

Transparent information is generally not in the long-run benefit of the corporation. We rest upon another theoretical perspective in our inquiry here, namely, that of collective action. Collective action theory (Olson 1965) states that there are shared public or "club" goods that are too expensive for any one person to provide, such as national security or mass transit. Arguably, the purpose of creating a government is to extract taxes in order to pay for such goods (Levi 1989); this is the idea behind the term "commonwealth." In some cases, a large group of powerful actors might be able to create a club good, such as a community pool. The challenge for such goods is the "free-rider" problem, whereby a tax evader, or a bus rider who refuses to pay the fare enjoys the public good without paying anything for it. Thus, one needs transparency and enforcement, such as random checks of bus riders to see if they have fare cards, or more generally, tax audits. The problem of collective action applies to CSR because a few businesses can "free ride" by not paying for information about reporting, or not reporting or enforcing standards to the same degree. Such activities are costly, so if there's no enforcement against free riders, it will be difficult for an industry or set of companies to convince the public they really are raising standards. As we discuss in later chapters, the collective goods of CSR are not delivered precisely because of the lack of transparency. With no way to really check up on them, businesses are free to continue to make bold claims about their contributions to sustainability; essentially CSR continues to be a self-reporting system. Transparency is essential for the enforcement necessary to collective action.

Bringing these elements together—the climate and inequality crises in global markets; the inability thus far to make adequate progress on the externality of climate change; information and power asymmetry on the side of corporations vis à vis governments and civil societies; and the absence of a system of collective enforcement to ensure uniform, transparent, and accountable CSR activities, we find ourselves boggled by the growing flurry of "responsible" activities and investments on the one hand, and the apparent reality of business as usual on the other. In fact, if we consider the "seven" proposed mechanisms of accountability: hierarchical; supervisory; fiscal; legal; market; peer; and public reputational (Grant and Keohane 2005), in the absence of global regulation, only the last three are potentially applicable to CSR on the global level in the absence of global authority. Yet, all three would strongly depend on transparency in information, and certainly are weak cousins to the other mechanisms necessary and available at the domestic level. While the US Securities and Exchange Commission can enforce financial reporting in New York, it has no control over the regulations in Mumbai. This leads to the last set of concepts around how global collective action is created.

The set of emerging theories around this action falls broadly under creating global "regimes" or "global governance" (Hira 2020a). Such theories readily acknowledge the limits of state power, but they posit that global markets work precisely because there are shared norms, rules, and principles (aka "regimes"), and that international organizations help to create and adapt and report on them. We say report, because there is no ability of international organizations to enforce rules. They don't have an audit agency or army or ability to enforce penalties on their side. So, global regime and governance theory suggest that they principally act as "brokers," bringing different global actors together for common cause. Common rules guide everyday transactions across the globe, from bank transfers to plane landings.

However, when it comes to CSR, there are far greater challenges, as we discuss in Chapter 2. To begin with, CSR lacks commonly agreed-upon concepts, metrics, or any ability for enforcement. Simply put, it mostly relies upon self-reporting by companies, or the inter-corporate agencies, international organizations, and audit agencies they hire to verify their CSR activities.

The preceding explains why we choose to focus on the CSR reporting system in this book. We acknowledge that it would be ideal to have a form of global government like a domestic agency that was democratically representative to create and enforce rules around corporate behavior, but there is no current prospect for such. Yet, the need for CSR is greater than ever given the multiple global crises we face; we simply can't leave it up to market forces to address collective action issues such as climate change. In this context, we posit that information is essential for accountability. Among other things, it can provide a "boomerang effect" for powerful Western actors (pension funds and activists) to more consistently and effectively push for genuine corporate social responsibility on the global level. This is analogous to the power posited of information of human rights abuses (Keck and Sikkink 2014). Activists can only hold companies to account if they know what they are doing. If linked to market access in the West, transparent and reliable information would be a foundation for accountability at last.

The fundamental effort in this book is to trace out how the most egregious human rights violations are reported in the current system. The exercise in our book may seem simplistic at first glance, but it reveals the fundamental and crucial limitations of the current CSR reporting system. We focus specifically on reporting mechanisms for SRI. While there are other promising catalysts for change, such as NGOs/activists/protests, media stories, shareholder activism, and legal suits, these are limited to individual cases, whereas SRI offers a global approach that potentially creates a new enforcement mechanism for improved environmental, labor, and social standards.[1]

Unlike the largely normative arguments of the traditional critical literature, SRI offers a strong market-based "club" to push for CSR information transparency and enforcement. It is based upon the increasingly recognized power of large pension funds to more directly sway corporate behavior through their investment decisions. Such pressures are converging with attempts to create more standardized reporting systems for non-financial matters, as we discuss below. Many of these pension funds represent large numbers of public sector union members, who are latent potential activists in their middle class and more empathetic orientation than corporate managers, policymakers, or investment brokers. If pension fund holders are willing to pressure their pension fund managers to push companies to reduce carbon emissions, improve labor standards, and pay their fair share of taxes, etc., the world can change.

---

1 For example, around the time of writing, the shareholder activism from a large pension fund manager was pushing Shell Oil to be far more aggressive in its climate transition plans. Around the same time, a Dutch court ordered the oil giant to move toward cutting emissions by 45% by 2030 from 2019 levels. See: https://www.theguardian.com/business/2021/may/24/influential-investor-joins-shareholder-rebellion-over-shells-climate-plan; and https://www.cbc.ca/news/canada/calgary/shell-dutch-court-ruling-emissions-1.6040842; both accessed October 29, 2021.

In short, the catalyst for our effort is to see the extent to which the CSR information system can start to guide this new generation of activist shareholders to push for corporate behavior to become more responsible. Any such transformation depends ultimately upon them having access to good information systems about what corporations are actually doing. So, we begin by examining the accuracy, accountability, and transparency of global reporting systems of corporate behavior. Then, we turn more pointedly to the reporting systems around SRI, particularly the increasingly important ratings systems provided by financial and accounting firms to provide clear information for SRI.

We do this by examining whether and how widely reported "adverse" events, such as mining disasters, flow through the SRI reporting systems. The following diagram reflects our empirical strategy:

Adverse events → Is the information found on the SRI reporting system? → Does the adverse event affect the SRI ratings negatively?

The exercise was not as simple as it appears. To begin with, there is, surprisingly, no authoritative objective source of information on adverse corporate events. We were, nonetheless, able to find a few good news aggregators and then started to create databases of multiple adverse events involving the same large multinational companies when reported by multiple sources. This gives us confidence that these adverse events were real and that information about them was globally accessible. Just as there are multiple reporting systems for CSR, by individual companies, industry clubs, international organizations, and NGOs, there are multiple reporting systems for SRI. We were able to gain access to reports of a few to check out the information flow for the adverse events we identified. The last challenge was to see what the ramifications were for the adverse events. Ideally, we would find that negative ratings led to pension fund managers pressuring corporations to change course and address the causes of the adverse outcomes. Unfortunately, we found that the CSR reporting system confounds and obfuscates, rather than illuminates, corporate activity.

In sum, through our exercise, we find that the CSR reporting system is incomplete, unaccountable, and has few discernible effects on either SRI investment activity or corporate behavior. We posit that a good CSR information system should have the following elements:

• Fully financed and comprehensive reporting systems that avoid conflicts of interest by reporters/auditors/evaluators with the companies or states they are assessing and are neutral in governance, including auditing and enforcement decisions

- Includes assessments of state as well as company activities, particularly around the use of revenues received from multinational companies, regulatory capacity, and activities; delivery and quality of public services, and examinations of local support for the state, such as through surveys and social science studies
- Meaningful stakeholder participation, including local populations, in ways that allow them to freely and anonymously voice their concerns and to organize where necessary to promote a change in policies
- Transparent and independent compliance reporting or enforcement systems for violations, including post hoc assessments of compliance and measurements of progress
- A means for safe appeals, complaints, and effective responses to violations
- A system to examine impacts and conditions more generally around human rights and environment, that ensures improvement in outcomes through follow-through and enforcement for accountability
- A system to ensure learning and improvement over time so that other companies/states/communities can learn from each other
- Extension of obligations to capacity building and enforcement by domestic authorities

Of course, simply creating a reliable information system will not solve all the problems of corporate malfeasance. As we report below, all reporting centers on the basic concept of "financial materiality," that is, any reporting has to relate to the possibilities to affect returns on investment. We certainly acknowledge that the average pensioner may not pay enough attention or care enough about climate change or workers overseas to pressure their money managers. However, the social movements literature, including the history of corporate scandals, tells us that a small group of activists can make a difference over time. After all, the modern CSR movement can be related to a series of scandals, such as those involving Nike, in the 1990s that brought media and activist attention and forced major new investments in CSR. In short, a robust information system can help to cauterize the different strands of activism toward a common purpose, one that is fully embraced by Western corporations. We just want these companies held to what they promise they are already doing. Pensioners do not need to follow the reporting system; they just need to pressure their money managers to do so.

Without a better, more standardized and accountable information system, CSR will remain in the realm of corporate self-reporting, with no real change in behavior or the ability to address the global issues caused in good part by corporate activities. CSR reform does not necessarily mean significant sacrifices to investors or pensioners. As we relate below, the studies on returns of ethical versus unconditional investment are ambiguous. More broadly, what good is a return if it brings climate change or migration waves that cost far more than an ounce of prevention? If child labor is unacceptable in the West, it should be so for the products consumers purchase that are made elsewhere. We believe that armed with more transparent information, vast amounts of capital will flow in more ethical directions; markets can work if they are transparent. Moreover, global regulation can only be constructed on the foundation of a robust reporting system. The occasional media scandal followed by superficial promises is quickly forgotten by the public (Hira 2017). Furthermore, investors and consumers can only act when they have reliable information about what corporations are actually doing. In fact, neither government nor civil society can do anything but continue to protest in the most general terms unless they are aware of the everyday decisions, actions, behavior, and consequences of corporations. In this book, we demonstrate that information truly is power.

Chapter 1

CORPORATE SOCIAL RESPONSIBILITY: A GOOD DEED IN NAME

Introduction

Corporate social responsibility (CSR) is the idea that corporations will choose to act ethically because it is in their interests to do so, both as good citizens and as a good business. CSR has deep roots in Western society, including nineteenth-century anti-slavery movements and religious groups' prohibitions on boycotts or investments in sinful production (Newholm et al. 2015). Early in the twentieth century, corporate philanthropy, such as that of Andrew Carnegie, reflected a growing conscience among corporate barons of the damaging effects of negative reputation, a tradition that continues today with splashy foundations by Bill Gates and Jeff Bezos. Many of the early large monopolists saw the interest of investing in basic social services for their workers; such is the provenance of many historical public projects, including universities and libraries. They were spurred on by "muckraking" journalist-activists such as Ida Tarbell who exposed Rockefeller's oil monopoly tactics and piqued elite consciences toward state action (Husted 2015). More fundamentally, the movement to make corporations more accountable to society is part of the broader "double movement" described by Polanyi (1944) as the main reason why leftist revolutions in the West universally failed. That is, Western society in the early twentieth century began to institute laws curbing the behavior of corporations, from antitrust to child labor to worker safety laws, with the idea that private purpose should fit within socially-acceptable parameters. Eventually, this came to include far-reaching state interventions, from social security to public health care. Such general evolutionary shifts in capitalistic relations reflected a "social pact" whereby corporations were willing to pay taxes on income so that they would have a healthy and well-educated workforce and consumers. The most important development was the rise of labor unions that created a strong force, over several decades in the early to mid-20th century, to counter corporate power in the court of the state. We should not exaggerate the sustainability of such movements, considering the subsequent deterioration of the pacts in recent decades.

In the 1970s, Milton Friedman brought to the table an important point about the limited nature of business responsibility, that is, that corporate managers are adept and skilled at their business, but not in other matters. Businesses should focus on making profits, for which they are designed. He points to the inherent ambiguity of defining corporate responsibility and where its bounds lie. Finally, he notes the underlying fiduciary responsibility that a manager has to their shareholders, fellow workers/bosses, and to their suppliers and customers (Friedman 1970). Such fundamental truths hold through to today and underlie much of the superficiality and evasiveness of CSR as currently practiced.

Countervailing forces to corporate power are hard to find these days; arguably, many states are "captured" by corporate interests, which explains, for example, the slow phaseout of fossil fuels. Furthermore, union power has declined precipitously across the West, for a variety of reasons ranging from "financialization" or the rise of the financial industry, along with offshore tax havens, to the shift from manufacturing to services and automation (Hira 2019). Regardless of the reasons, the proportionate power of corporations vis à vis states and civil society has grown enormously, fueled by globalization, which allows for evasion from domestic regulations, as seen in the "offshoring" of jobs and profits (Hira and Hira 2005). Indeed, corporate behavior in terms of environmental and labor standards overseas remains largely unregulated.

While we generally consider the value of a "brand" as tied to corporate behavior, the implications of corporate social responsibility are conceived by experts and practitioners as much wider in terms of "corporate citizenship" or corporations as key "stakeholders" in society. The collective interests of corporations to behave responsibly should, in theory, follow from such. For example, environmental destruction leading to climate change will threaten a wide range of economic activity, injuring corporations other than those directly involved in fossil fuels or tied to them, such as autos. In fact, in the wake of the 2008 financial crisis and the multiple issues flagged around the financial industry reporting (Hira et al. 2019), along with climate change, there has been a larger push across business scholarship to research and train ethics in business. Yet, without global policies, collective action to address issues such as basic worker safety and climate change have flagged behind stated intentions.

Recognizing that there are individual episodes of corporations seeking to act responsibly, ethical scandals abound, from reporting about Amazon's working conditions to oil company funding of climate change denial.[1] Indeed, according to the limited datasets available, there has been no discernible

---

1 Examples include Michael Sainato, 2020, "'I'm Not a Robot': Amazon Workers Condemn Unsafe, Grueling Conditions at Warehouse." *The Guardian*. Feb. 5. Available

reduction in corporate scandals over the past two decades (Hira 2020a). One can argue instead that CSR is a way for business to avoid further regulation and taxation by heading off social movements, no different than the philanthropy projects of the early twentieth-century robber barons.

The problem is fundamentally one of incentives. While many scholars posit that corporations have a clear interest in good behavior (Carroll and Shabana, 2010), it's hard to sustain such an argument when ethical actions are clear and costly, while payback is obtuse and uncertain. As Friedman observed, the overriding logic of corporations is profit maximization, which may lead to quite different calculations than social responsibility-driven behavior. Executive compensation and indices of success are based largely upon share prices; it is inevitable that profit will usurp ethical decisions that are not in line with it. Unless there is a tangible payoff for good behavior, corporations will most likely act in a hesitant and minimal way, protecting the bottom line for themselves and their shareholders, which is their stated mission. In short, the idea that CSR is good for the bottom line in any demonstrable way is dubitable.

In the West, corporations have traditionally been bound by domestic regulation. Even here continuing issues raise doubts about the efficacy and independence of regulators, such as the inability to put in place sensible policy solutions to the climate crisis, such as a carbon tax. Even leading climate change states, such as Germany, have struggled to close down coal plants and are now increasing natural gas as fast as renewables. More importantly, globalization reduces the power of domestic policy. The well-publicized offshoring of profits, leading to many large corporations paying minimal (or zero) rates of taxes, is but one example of the limits of regulation. Labor standards remain atrocious in many global factories that make our clothes and electronics.

In light of regulatory failures at both the national and global levels, non-state actors, particularly NGOs/activists and labor unions, have pushed for greater corporate responsibility. The main channel has been publicity through the media and, more recently, efforts to affect corporate boards through shareholder activism. Such efforts have yielded some isolated victories. However, longer-term "structural" issues such as labor standards and climate change seem immune to these channels of accountability. Understandably, the episodic nature of scandal-based accountability mechanisms fails to lead to any sustained or systematic response.

---

at: https://www.theguardian.com/technology/2020/feb/05/amazon-workers-protest-unsafe-grueling-conditions-warehouse, Accessed Sept. 27, 2021; The Climate Reality Project, 2019, "The Climate Denial Machine: How the Fossil Fuel Industry Blocks Climate Action," Available at: https://www.climaterealityproject.org/blog/climate-denial-machine-how-fossil-fuel-industry-blocks-climate-action, Accessed Sept. 27, 2021.

On the domestic level, there are nascent efforts at regulating corporate disclosures to reveal ethical (non-financial) activities (Hebb et al. 2015) and climate change that would be a big step forward. However, these efforts are so far haphazard, and it's unclear how they will be enforced or followed through. On the global level, the lack of regulation around CSR beyond voluntary principled agreements, such as the Global Compact, reveals the lack of accountability, transparency, and enforcement of corporate norms. *The one axe that societies and governments have to promote CSR revolves around whether to invest in companies.* Companies require a regular influx of capital to carry out their activities, and the success of their CEOs is often measured by share price, reflecting investment interest and the continual need for access to capital. Not surprisingly, they are very responsive to shifts in investment, and more specifically to the large pools of capital controlled by large investment and pension funds, upon which they rely for investment capital and share prices.

Socially responsible investment (SRI) is an increasingly important factor in global finance. SRI guides huge pools of capital tied to pension funds, whose often public sector members want to feel ethical about the use of their pooled savings. Pools of pension funds are among the most important concentrations of capital and, along with shareholder activism, have the ability to directly influence corporate decision-making based on ethical principles. Friede et al. (2015) estimate that approximately $60 trillion, or 50% of total global institutional assets, are managed under the Principles for Responsible Investment. A Massachusetts Institute of Technology (MIT) project states that the portion of global assets invested based on ESG (environment, social, and governance assessments of company performance) ratings has increased by 34% since 2016.[2] A raft of business authors such as Balkin (2016), seeing such actions, posit once again that there is no contradiction in the premise that companies can "do well, by doing good." This is reflected in activism by large fund shareholders, who are increasingly making demands on corporate governance, such as increasing diversity or reducing carbon emissions (McCahery et al. 2016).

Ultimately, SRI pension fund managers depend upon information to make responsible investment decisions. The primary information system consists of two parts: the first is a patchwork of global reporting regimes, which we review in Chapter 2, and the second is subscription-based ratings agencies

---

2 https://mitsloan.mit.edu/sustainability-initiative/aggregate-confusion-project, Accessed July 26, 2021.

designed precisely for the SRI market, to which we turn in Chapter 3. Before we get to the reporting, we begin with a brief introduction to CSR and why its very core is contradictory and problematic.

Corporate Motivations for CSR Are Ambiguous as Is the Potential for CSR in Governance

No Clear Definition of CSR

Corporate social responsibility has deep historical roots in Western conscience. Religious beliefs swayed some Christian organizations to proscribe working with companies with ties to the slave trade as far back as the eighteenth century. Other groups avoided investments in companies involved in the business of sin, including gambling, tobacco, and alcohol (Brill and Rader 1993).

Such ideas were limited for most of the twentieth century. Theodore Levitt suggested that 'government's job is not business, and business's job is not government' (1958, 47). Davis (1973) also held that businesses did not have competence in pursuing social objectives. In short, the dominant approach in business was (and remains) to focus on financial return. Compliance with legal statutes including liability is the true extent of a company's social responsibility; its primary responsibility is to its shareholders.

The modern notion of CSR seems to date back to the 1990s, when long-standing ideas about the limits on corporate responsibility began to be challenged. The general shift toward CSR built upon the momentum created by the global divestment work in response to South African apartheid, beginning in the 1970s; the eventual success of such unleashed a new era in activism. Ascending from the late 1990s, the publicity around abysmal factory conditions such as those related to Nike and Kathie Lee Gifford's clothing line for Walmart was the push for more formal, industry-wide standards. The "discovery" of a sweatshop outside of Los Angeles (El Monte) in 1995 with slave-like working conditions led President Clinton to develop the Apparel Industry Partnership to improve labor standards (Ross 2004, 161). In 1998, a number of major apparel firms in the United States and NGOs developed a code of conduct through the Fair Labor Association to monitor in certifying companies to meet labor standards through the Apparel Industry Partnership. Similar campaigns took place in the Netherlands with the Clean Clothes Campaign, in the United Kingdom with the Ethical Trading Initiative, and in Australia with the Fair Wear Campaign. Most companies have adopted social affairs departments to deal with such issues.

While some analysts hold that such codes have made a significant difference, there are no systematic data on the topic. There is no central registry or tracking of codes. Attempts to harmonize codes have been ineffective (Madhav 2012, 282; Hira 2020a).

From these modest and haphazard beginnings, a more intricate system of CSR has emerged. The literature on institutional origins (Scott 2014) points to both "natural" and agent-based approaches to how institutions come into being (114). "Institutional entrepreneurs" are those who find new ways to combine resources, both human and technical, and/or ways to change rules, norms, or belief systems to create new action (117). In the United States, the social and civil rights movements of the 1960s changed perceptions, and led to a host of new regulatory agencies, such as the Environmental Protection Agency, the Consumer Product Safety Commission, and the Equal Employment Opportunity Commission. In 1980, President Reagan reversed such momentum in shifting toward what is now known as neoliberalism, which suggests that the private sector is better equipped to handle social issues, such as privatized infrastructure (public–private partnerships), where the benefits of competition and competence outweigh distortionary public regulation and social purpose. The deregulation and privatization movement went hand in hand with the acceptance of stakeholder theory that businesses need to think about a number of constituents, including workers, customers, subcontractors, and local communities (Freeman 1984), paradoxically presenting these stakeholders as an extension of customers with implications for purchasing decisions and thereby the bottom line. Even governments adopted the "new public management" whereby they began to see citizens as clients. By the 1990s, CSR had become largely accepted as an idea and spread to the global activities of corporations and to include concerns around sustainability (Carroll 2015). This is reflected in the vast acceleration in CSR reporting as well as in numerous advertisements lauding corporate good behavior and beneficence, such as British Petroleum's "beyond petrol" campaign.

Business scholars increasingly insist that CSR is good for business, and its growing importance is reflected in the spread of ethics topics across business curricula. Carroll and Shabana (2010, 88–89) suggest that there are a number of arguments for CSR. First, by contributing, business will ensure a healthy environment in which to operate. Second, it can avoid additional government regulation. Third is the idea that business has managerial talent and expertise that give it unusual competencies for solving nagging social issues. Last but not least is that the public now expects corporations to contribute. Like others, van Marrewijk (2003, 100) sees CSR as part of a triangular relationship among the state, businesses, and civil society.

The state legislates and regulates, businesses create efficient goods through competition, and civil society structures that competition through demand and participation. Mirvis and Googins (2006) argue that CSR drivers are primarily internal rather than external, based on corporate values and motivations. Kanter (1999) sees CSR as a form of product differentiation, while Porter and Kramer (2011) suggest philanthropy gives companies a competitive edge in positioning their products.

One can posit that CSR places a general core of ethical notions as important to guide corporate behavior, as reflected in the series of global agreements that we discuss below. However, the definition of CSR remains rather fuzzy. Dahlsrud (2006) counts at least 37 different definitions. Carroll's (1991) famous pyramid suggests that there are four different kinds of CSR: economic, legal, ethical, and philanthropic, with each level being a higher place on the pyramid, representing less important but still desirable goals. Economic refers to the normal functions of a corporation to deliver goods at an efficient and profitable rate. Ethical responsibilities extend legal obligations to the social normative plane. The expectation is that CSR demonstrates good citizenship and improves corporate reputation. Aguinis (2011) offers an approach that begins to incorporate sustainability notions, suggesting that CSR constitutes "context-specific organizational actions and policies that take into account stakeholders' expectations and the triple bottom line of economic, social, and environmental performance."

To further illustrate the ambiguity around the extent to which CSR exists and why, Doane (2005) posits that corporate responsibility initiatives can be ascribed to four key motivations: managing risk and reputation, protecting capital assets, responding to consumer demands, and avoiding regulation. Wood, (1991, 604) meanwhile, suggests the need for general legitimacy as an institution of society, a responsibility to the public, and the responsibility of individual managers to act upon these. This ambiguity of purpose extends to the empirical literature. In a survey of Mexican auto parts suppliers, for example, Muller and Kolk (2010) find that the social values of individual managers make a major difference in the level of CSR. On a broader level, some authors (e.g. Scherer and Palazzo 2011) see CSR as a natural development that is part of a general shift toward deliberative democracy.

Even with the best of intentions, CSR is a governance conundrum. There are natural concerns that if only one subset of companies pursues CSR, they will be put at a competitive disadvantage against those who do not. Thus, absent a global system of regulation, the current arrangements ultimately rely upon voluntary corporate adoption of ethical principles and self-enforcement (Hira 2020a). It is not too fanciful to suggest that we may be witnessing a slow evolution toward the development of institutions around CSR that would codify and enforce rules around a genuine governance system. However, until they are up and running, the main arguments for CSR have to rely on the idea that voluntarily responsible behavior is good for corporations' bottom line, a dubitable proposition at best, as we have just demonstrated. In the following sections, we further unpack the contested notions for why companies pursue CSR, finding each wanting.

No Profit Incentives for CSR

As Brooks and Oikonomou (2018) point out in their review of the empirical literature examining the impact of CSR on firm value, there are confounding results for several reasons: differences in definitions of CSR and financial performance, differences in theoretical frameworks and hypotheses, differences in datasets and variables, and differences in econometric methodologies. While the authors posit an "economically modest" link between CSR and financial performance, they note that the shape of the relationship between the two is unclear.

Indeed, whether CSR improves corporate profitability is at best contentious based on a large number of empirical studies; thus, no CEO or board can clearly see incentives for truly embracing ethical shifts that might negatively affect the bottom line. Natural caution outside of specifically responsible branding such as fair trade coffee or Patagonia clothing, for which ethics is a key selling point, is not surprising given the number of factors, many difficult to discern, that might impact profits. The plethora of responsibility-claiming advertisement campaigns and some research suggest that CSR affects corporate and brand reputations through customer perceptions and loyalty (Markovic et al. 2018; Kim 2019). Yet this leads us to recognize the value of corporate campaigns to show that they are doing good, rather than concrete activities or outcomes (that they are actually doing good).

In examining both the direct and indirect effects, empirical studies reach confounding conclusions about whether CSR is really good for the bottom line (profit). On the one hand, Waddock and Graves (1997) find a positive relationship through mediating variables, such as innovation, human resources, reputation, and corporate culture. On the other hand, Vogel (2010, 82) states that CSR is "irrelevant" to the bottom line. Surroca et al. (2010) find no relationship between CSR and financial performance. Still other studies argue, by contrast, that the relationship between CSR and profitability is negative, based upon increases in costs (López et al. 2007). Hong and Kacperczyk (2009), in turn, find that returns to "sin" sectors such as alcohol and tobacco are higher; thus, there is a financial penalty for ethical investing.

Gimenez et al. (2012) conclude in an international study of manufacturing firms that environmental measures are positive for the bottom line, while social measures likely involve higher costs.

More recent literature reinforces doubts about the link between CSR and financial performance. For example, Bae et al. (2021), examining Morgan Stanley Capital International (MSCI) and Refinitiv scores, find no relationship between CSR scores and stock market prices during the COVID-19 pandemic. Hawn et al. (2018), examining the Dow Jones Sustainability World Index (DJSI), find that major events in the index have only "limited significance and/or materiality." Similarly, Nguyen et al. (2020), separating long-term from short-term investors (based on the percentage of annual portfolio turnover) against KLD CSR data from 1991 to 2009, find *no* effect of long-term investment horizons (which presumably will increase CSR accountability) on profits of companies but find that profit variability decreases. They conclude that CSR can help profitability "as long as managers are properly monitored by long-term investors." Awaysheh et al. (2020) control for industry, separating out best in class from worst in class companies by the CSR score in the DJSI index but find *no* relationship between CSR performance and financial return.

Beyond the mixed results around whether CSR is profitable lies a trove of empirical, correlational studies around what firm characteristics spur greater ESG activity. In a wide-ranging review of the literature, Gillan et al. (2021) find, for example, that firms operating in Northern markets with significant institutional investor ownership and diverse boards are more likely to engage in ESG reporting, not surprisingly. However, the authors reflect on the limitations of the research methodology of the large statistical studies that predominate in the CSR space. They conclude:

> There are several common trends in the results across papers we have reviewed that do not have clear explanations regarding the mechanisms through which these trends arise [...]. Disparities exist as well across different research studies on the same central topics [...]. Disparities also exist in the results across studies of ownership structure [...]. Across the ESG/CSR literature and within studies, some of the disparate results appear to be related to differences in how ESG/CSR performance is measured (e.g. an aggregate measure of a firm's ESG/CSR profile, a specific sub-measure, or a focus on a particular issue such as corporate charitable donations, etc), the particular data-set that is used, and the geographic focus. Thus, the extent to which certain aspects of ESG/CSR drive the empirical findings remains an open issue [...]. Importantly, ESG/CSR studies vary widely in their definitions of key

explanatory variables of interest [...]. Finally, researchers continue to face the challenge of establishing causality when focusing on aspects of corporate finance and ESG/CSR performance. Clearly, additional methodologies and approaches to deal with this issue are needed.

Matching the lack of clear data or demonstrated variables, there are increasing questions around CSR efficacy. For example, Kraus et al. (2020) find that the level of CSR reporting does not have any effect on the environmental performance of 297 manufacturing firms in Malaysia, though they hold it might have an "indirect" influence in spurring green innovation. Similar to the findings we present below, Aouadi and Marsat (2018) find that ESG controversies have *no* impact on firm market value across 4,000 firms from 58 countries during 2002–2011. Drempetic et al. (2020), using the *Thompson Reuters* ASSET4 database, find that larger firms tend to have higher resources, concluding previous literature demonstrates "that sustainability ratings can positively influence investor's behavior. But does the capital really flow to sustainable businesses? If an ESG score depends mostly on the firm's size and resources, it challenges how comparable the sustainability is between different sectors and portfolios."

Questionable Benefits through Consumer Responses

The lack of clarity extends to potential secondary benefits of CSR in the realm of consumer perceptions that would lead to increases in purchase. For example, some suggest CSR improves customer loyalty and trust (Aguinis and Glavas 2012), but there is no general proof of such a relationship. Mohr et al. (2001) find that there is a small group of consumers who are conscientious, willing to actively consider CSR in purchasing decisions. Similarly, Maignan et al. (1999) find that CSR increases both customer and employee loyalty. Bénabou and Tirole (2010) suggest that CSR is related to deeper psychological patterns behind human behavior, namely the need for status recognition. According to their review of psychological findings, social behavior is constrained and guided by the expected perceptions of others; thus, shaming is important but so is the recognition of good deeds. Good deeds confer a sense of social status, especially to those who are ahead of the pack, such as the first producer of a hybrid car (Toyota with the Prius). Thus, visibility is an important part of CSR, and this matches with the literature about CSR as a branding mechanism. Branding a product as part of a socially responsible lifestyle will not necessarily be backed up by true responsibility; in the absence of clear information about production along the supply chain, consumers may be convinced by slick marketing.

For example, a green product may be created with poor labor practices or with limited postconsumer recyclability, with no way for the consumer to really even know whether the green claim is true.

Yet, other studies raise serious doubts about whether a responsive consumer relationship consistently exists (McWilliams and Siegel 2000; Luo and Bhattacharya 2006). Many scholars point out that general consumer awareness of CSR efforts is really lacking (Pomering and Dolnicar 2009; Servaes and Tamayo 2013). In sum, the question of whether a mass group of consumers will respond positively to ethical choices by a company as part of a branding exercise remains very much in doubt (Tarabashkina et al. 2020).

Based upon past responsiveness to corporate scandals, such as those around sweatshop allegations, a small group of activists can make a difference, but only for a short window. For example, the scandals around Nike in the 1990s forced it to adopt a more active corporate responsibility stance, similar to the scandals around Apple in the last decade. The difference has come on occasion where large groups of consumers or large institutional customers make a stand against a brand (Seidman 2007, 133). However, these are retrograde, defensive actions in response to a specific scandal, eliciting a specific response with no long-term follow-through. As Locke (2013) points out in his extensive study of Nike audits, the system put in place in the wake of such scandals had ephemeral effects in terms of assuring labor standards. Similarly, Apple continues to be rocked by labor scandals and unrest at its Foxconn partner factories in China. In November 2022, for example, worker strikes threatened Apple's ability to supply iPhones for the holiday shopping season (Lee 2022).

CSR Isomorphism as a Cultural Phenomenon

Several scholars find CSR in practice tends toward a form of corporate isomorphism (mimetic behavior) following the example of a company introducing related competing products or services or similar responses to similar challenges (DiMaggio and Powell 1983; Husted and Allen 2006). Isomorphism can also be a more automatic imitation with companies seeing CSR as part of an overall successful formula by competitors. Over time, as CSR becomes "normalized," it is adopted without question, as not doing so would be considered illegitimate or even deviant behavior (Scott 2014, 185, 203).

Following this line of reasoning, both the varieties of capitalism (Hall and Gingerich 2009) and the historical institutional approaches (Farrell and Newman 2010) emphasize differences in CSR, reflecting differences in the way that the US and European economies are set up. Maignan et al. (1999) find higher levels of expectations for CSR among European survey respondents versus US ones. Waldman et al. (2006) find that not only cultural values but also visionary leadership matter in the degree to which companies practice CSR. Cultural values such as egalitarianism and collectivism lead to greater CSR. The differential role of governments, the media, and NGO observers has been well documented. For example, Marquis and Qian (2014) find that Chinese companies are far more likely to engage in CSR when there is government monitoring. This reinforces the fact that isomorphism has only a limited effect; a firmer institutional basis for CSR to become effective practice is needed.

Institutional Pressures: Unrealized Potential

Institutional theories of CSR suggest that social environment shapes corporate behavior. One typology sees three different forces. The first is coercion of the state. The second is the effects of the market organization upon firm policies and structures. The third is internal policies and practices within the organization itself (Fligstein 1991). Another well-cited typology (Scott 2014) suggests that three different forces push companies into CSR: cultural cognitive or shared frameworks of interpretation, social normative or shared values for appropriate behavior, and regulative or formal and informal constraints on action. The institutional approach effectively sees corporations as a different type of citizen-actor, with rights and responsibilities. However, the literature does not explain how such responsibilities are to be enforced.

A growing number of authors point to shareholder and investor activism as sources of CSR. For example, Kang and Moon (2012) suggest that national institutional arrangements allow different levels and types of stakeholder engagement, thus resulting in different levels of CSR and explaining variation across the United States and European Union (EU). Increasing stakeholder pressure, from corporate boards, the media, the local community, and activist groups is increasingly acknowledged as a motivating factor behind CSR (Aguinis and Glavas 2012). The potentially game changing force of SRI and its ability to affect the bottom line make it the subject of our subsequent investigation.

Conclusion

Figure 1.1 summarizes the relationships among actors that lead to CSR activities as reflected in our review of the literature.

By contrast with SRI, brand reputation is in practice a quite limited incentive. While there may be a few outliers related to setting up ethics as part of the corporate brand, such as Patagonia, which supports lifetime use of its clothing, these are the exception. Outside of a passing scandal that elicits lip service promises of drastic change, as we detail in our cases below, the fundamental environmental, labor, and social issues across global

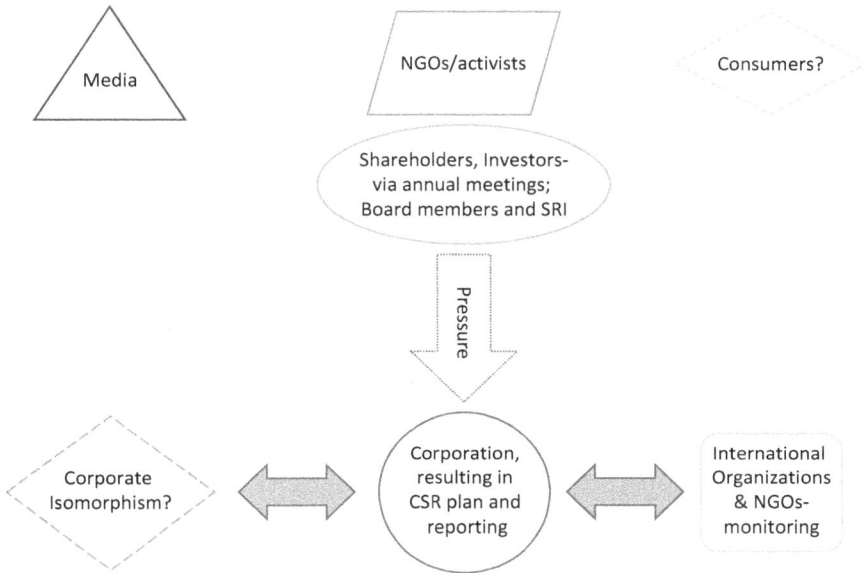

Figure 1.1 Corporate Social Responsibility (CSR) Motivations.

production remain unaddressed. Customers, by and large, are *not* (thus far) demanding better choices in a way that would affect company decisions, except in very select niche markets, such as those for fair trade. Most advertising and branding do *not* have any explicit ethical content or seek to demonstrate ethical behavior, thus reflecting its general lack of importance to purchasers. Price points and quality/branding attributes remain the main criteria for whether to buy. One of the barriers to customer activation is the lack of consensus and transparency about what is ethical. Any number of standards from Utz to various fair trade claims to Rainforest Alliance, etc. pepper labels alongside ubiquitous company declarations of their own ethical behavior. Outside a small niche of consumers willing to pay attention and generally to pay an ethical premium, it has not changed the bulk of the marketplace, reflecting fragmentation and fundamental weaknesses in ethical purchasing, starting with the idea of creating "pure" alternative supply chains and minimum prices (Hira and Ferrie 2006).

Of all the different possible reasons for CSR that we have reviewed, besides SRI, only shareholder activism has a clear, tangible, and direct potential to have an effect on the profitability of a company. Even here, there are major reasons to doubt any systematic action toward ethical behavior enforcement among corporations. Activist shareholders, by definition, have to be large holders of capital, and thus are highly unlikely to have perspectives of marginalized groups.

Sandberg's (2011) review of attempts by shareholder activists at board meetings concludes that they are largely ineffective in changing corporate agendas. The laws and power structures around corporate governance systems prevent a minority from wielding any influence beyond making a statement at an Annual General Meeting. These include restrictions on time for filing and voting on shareholder resolutions; limitations on the potential scope of resolutions, such as viewing discrimination as an HR matter; the need to circulate resolutions among all shareholders, when who they are is generally unknown, unless the company did so, which is extremely unlikely; and the fact that voting is usually proscribed from interfering with company operations or investment decisions. As Sandberg notes, a company's practices reflect a set of management values, and singular resolutions with no teeth of enforcement are hardly likely to change corporate cultures. At the time of writing, there is a seed of hope for enacting standards in the West for ethical behavior of Western corporations abroad, such as the 2021 Dutch court ruling for Shell's liability around oil spills in Nigeria. For now, the greatest hope lies in public union pension funds, who, via SRI, open the possibility that the worker members may be sympathetic toward negative social, labor, and environmental effects of corporate activity and force investment decisions to shift accordingly.

The reality for now is that, in the absence of significant and sustained consumer or investor pressure and global regulation, companies have devised their own systems of ethical compliance. Pressures for compliance come from changes in internal norms but more importantly from global activists and activist shareholders. One of the leading authors on CSR, Archie B. Carroll (2021), states that sustainability and human rights are important frontiers for CSR reporting, concluding, "the field needs to move beyond just 'respecting' human rights and get into proactive company involvement in protecting and realizing human rights." Compliance can only come with a robust reporting system that incentivizes and rewards CSR investment, reveals free riders, and provides lessons for improving social and environmental outcomes.

The empirical work in this book focuses on how the CSR reporting system currently reflects serious human rights violations by Western companies, to test the responses to the most extreme event, deaths from corporate activity. Reinforcing the literature, we find that CSR reporting is not tied to actual performance. As Barnett et al. (2020) conclude in their meta-study of the CSR literature, "Thus, after an extensive analysis of the thousands of studies populating the CSR–performance literature, we find that the literature has advanced, but we do not find a single study that adequately demonstrates that CSR initiatives resolved the social problems they intended to address." The rest of this book examines how and where accountability and transparency systems in CSR reporting break down, before turning to how they can be fixed.

Chapter 2

THE SHELL GAME OF GLOBAL CSR REPORTING

Global Reporting as the Solution to the Corporate Collective Action Problem

The Collective Action Problem

While the motivations behind corporate social responsibility (CSR) are unclear and mixed, there is no denying that corporations are increasingly engaged in CSR activities. Foremost, they see the need to avoid scandals that will affect the value of their brand from global activists, reduce their attractiveness to investment managers, and potentially bring lawsuits and/ or regulation. However, CSR activities and enforcement, even if internal, are costly, especially when considered as part of a set of industry activities. On top of this, one bad clothing or mining company can spoil the reputation of an entire industry. The problem of CSR thus fits into the classic "collective action" problem as described by Olson (1965). Olson points out that some "public" goods, such as national defense, are too expensive for any one actor to provide and their benefits are not excludable. This implies the need for government to raise taxes and fund public goods. However, most goods are excludable, even if they are "lumpy" or too expensive for an individual actor to afford. These are "club" or shared private goods. If there is a large enough group of wealthy actors who can coordinate, they may be able to provide enough resources for a club good that no one individual alone can afford, such as a country club or a private housing development. In either the case of public or club goods, there has to be transparency and enforcement in terms of compliance and levels of support, in order to avoid the "free-rider" problem whereby a member reneges on its fair dues or the rules. CSR activities of an individual company are constantly likely to be undercut both by competitors who do not adopt the same standards and by companies who create scandals in the same industry through merely rhetorical adoption of standards, thus creating a huge free rider problem.

For example, as Nike and Apple have been accused of labor scandals, consumers and governments have become increasingly skeptical of all clothing and shoe and electronic companies. In this situation, the largest global brands have the most to lose.

Regimes as a Solution

CSR is increasingly seen as a "club good," whose costs are to be shared by the largest corporations and organized around regimes. Regimes come in the form of creating a set of rules, principles, and norms, along with enforcement provisions. Regime enforcement tends to rely on public reporting and technical assistance (Kirton and Trebilcock 2004, 9–23). Regimes are essentially self-enforced, and thus do not approach governmental authority (Krasner 1983). Regimes are often referred to as "soft law," to reflect a lack of reliance on state authority and their voluntary nature. Corporate regimes are often referred to as "private regimes" (Haufler 1999), to differentiate them from state-based regimes, such as the World Health Organization, where governments cooperate around a collective global good. Private firms can pool funding and expertise to resolve transparency and enforcement issues. Kirton and Trebilcock (2004, 5) suggest that there are serious advantages to soft law initiatives: the ability to move forward when states/international organizations (IOs) are stalemated; the ability to bring legitimacy, expertise, and other resources for creating new norms and standards; and an effective means to direct civil society participation.

There is now a panoply of private regimes around standards, such as the Forest Stewardship Council and the Social Accountability International (SAI) sets of standards, many of which are sector-specific. Corporations have to step up because there is no credible global authority to provide collective goods in the form of improved labor, environmental, and social standards (Cashore et al. 2004). The idea is that through transparent commitments, companies will adhere to the principles and standards that the club has agreed to, and not undercut each other. The private regime literature suggests that non-state actors, companies, sometimes with the help of NGOs and states, set up a "mixed regime" to change and direct global behavior.

However, the appearance of multiple private CSR regimes, many overlapping across sectors or countries, does not solve the problem of collective action. Since CSR standards do not require membership, there are many free riders. Moreover, there is no hard incentive for compliance, and transparency is limited since most data are self-reported. Companies face increasing reporting burdens by joining multiple standards regimes. Even where companies could agree upon a common set of rules, the lack of any authority for running the regime has created problems. Thus, private regimes continue to lead to companies being peppered with claims of hypocrisy by activists. For example, Knox et al. (2005) find in a survey of the top 150 Financial Times Stock Exchange (FTSE) companies that while larger companies are apt to pay more attention to CSR, all companies tend to do so in a reporting manner, rather than engaging in a direct way with concerned stakeholders. Delmas and Burbano (2011) go even further, suggesting that companies sometimes engage in "greenwashing," or putting forth false and/or misleading statements about the sustainable production and operation of their products and services. As Whitehouse (2006, 294), who conducted a study of leading UK companies on CSR, put it, "It would seem, therefore, that while managers, literally, cannot afford to ignore the issue of CSR, they can continue to define it in whatever manner best suits the interests of their company."

The solution that has evolved to address the lack of transparency or enforcement has been to create "mixed regimes" or "multi-stakeholder initiatives" (MSIs). These are systems of corporations that agree upon collective standards for their club, and then bring in IOs and NGOs to help them to create transparent rules and verify their enforcement. Like private regimes, the carrot for compliance is the ability to use a "seal" of approval by the regime. In a 2010 article, Abbott and Snidal call this "international regulation without international government." Figure 2.1 summarizes the evolution of the global CSR reporting regime in response to the collective action problems described above.

Figure 2.1 Evolutionary Layers of CSR Reporting.
Source: Author.

Mixed Regimes: How International Organizations and NGOs Legitimize Corporate Behavior

In mixed regimes, non-profit actors, such as NGOs or civil society organizations (CSOs), as well as public actors, namely, IOs, such as the United Nations (UN), gain a place at the table, as authorities in a position to both design and enforce global rules around corporate behavior. In return, corporations are able to add a strong sense of legitimacy to CSR efforts through claiming that a neutral party is verifying their compliance with ethical standards. The first main initiative was The Global Compact, founded in 2000.

Green and Auld (2017, 268–73, 283–84) posit that there are several payoffs for private/non-state actors to construct a mixed regime: it may provide and help incubate new ideas for solving the collective action problem; it provides an institution for addressing common issues; and it helps to create and harmonize rules for behavior. They also note important differences with public regimes: the proponents are non-state actors, mostly those in a particular economic sector; rules are voluntary; participants are subject to high turnover in line with the fortunes of individual companies; and rules are more easily modified as they are less negotiated and codified. However, they caution about the possibility that private or mixed regimes may crowd out public regulation.

Figure 2.1 demonstrates the mixed regime bargain. The Compact and similar international agreements are a win-win situation, where the IO/NGO receives recognition as an authoritative body, along with funding, and the company receives the good label of acceptance of its practices by a supposedly neutral global institution, thus reassuring governments, investors, NGO/activities, and consumers. By having a neutral party verify their behavior, they also resolve the collective action issue of self-verification by individual companies and thus provide a club incentive for companies to join, thus spreading the norms and rules as part of normal corporate practice, at least in theory [...].

As Zalik and Osuoka (2020) point out, mixed regimes came about in response to a series of scandals around the oil and mining sectors in the early 2000s, including ongoing allegations of corruption, environmental disasters, mining conflicts, and a growing sense of exasperation with the lack of clear development progress from extractive industries. Corporations joined with civil society actors, such as Publish What You Pay and the Global Reporting Initiative (GRI), in order to save their reputations. There is laudable progress from such efforts in regard to bringing corporate revenue contributions to transparency, thus reducing questions about company bribery of states by bringing transparency to revenue payments, and in turn, improving the negotiating power of states with weak capacity by allowing them to know the general terms of agreements with companies. Beyond the financial reporting are the increasingly important indicators of *ESG* (environmental, social, and governance) which are defined and reported in a highly varied number of ways across regimes, and are often sector-specific.

However, the dizzying array of reporting standards across different regimes underscores their voluntary and uneven nature (Hira 2020a). Equally problematic is the fact that they separate out overall performance based on financial reporting from environmental, social, human rights, and community development. Audits done by NGOs/consultants and IOs are uneven, inconsistent, and generally narrowly focused, and NGO reporting itself lacks validity, reliability, or accountability. NGOs depend on funding for their operations, so such reporting is tainted by the basic conflict of interest that a company is paying the auditor, paralleling similar issues in financial reporting leading up to the 2008 financial crisis, when rating agencies highly overvalued financial securities (Hira 2013), or by the NGOs' need to raise funds. Tang et al. (2021) conduct an econometric analysis testing this very question. They find ESG ratings on companies with the same owners as the raters receive higher ratings but have worse future ESG outcomes. There are simply too many apparent conflicts of interest between auditors/raters and the companies they are evaluating.

The issues run deeper still. Koenig-Archibugi and Macdonald (2017) suggest that one of the larger issues in the emerging RIT (Regulator, Intermediary, and Target, based on Abbott and Snidal (2010)) systems is the lack of participation of beneficiaries in the decision-making and auditing processes. Swyngedouw (2005) warns "the socially innovative figures of horizontally organized stakeholder arrangements of governance that appear to empower civil society in the face of an apparently overcrowded and 'excessive' state, may, in the end, prove to be the Trojan Horse that diffuses and consolidates the 'market' as the principal institutional form." They refer to civil society tokenism, where the appearance of consultation is made without any real consequences. As an example, the author discussed mining issues with a civil society roundtable in a Latin American country that was mandated by the country's need to comply with the Extractive Industries Transparency Initiative (EITI). The group had registered a series of human rights complaints with the EITI Secretariat and the government that were ignored, an all too common situation of civilian participation without meaningful consequences.

General CSR enforcement by IOs and NGOs has been widely registered as "going through the motions." Monitoring visits are often announced beforehand, and NGOs generally have not worked with local trade unions to develop regulatory capacity within host countries (Lane and Probert 2009, 283). Seidman (2007, 138) concludes in a review of post-audit conditions that "voluntary, privatized monitoring has had very little impact on working conditions." Companies who do not wish to change will gravitate toward monitors or NGOs who are more compliant. The Ethical Trading Initiative (website, "Auditing working conditions," accessed November 11, 2014), concludes

> the predominant approaches to auditing that companies have adopted, which typically involve commissioning third-party auditors to carry out inspections, followed by 'corrective action plans', fail to deliver any real change to workers' lives. Instead, the value of auditing has been undermined by low-quality inspections, poor value for money, unnecessary duplication of audits, inconsistent corrective action plans and, perhaps more worryingly, a rapid growth in 'audit fraud'. In fact, audit fraud is now so common that a whole new industry has developed to facilitate it.

Egels-Zandén and Lindholm (2015, 31) find that while auditing outcomes tend to improve over iterations, the overall performance in regard to basic worker rights, such as right of association and freedom of discrimination, does not, concluding that auditing is "fundamentally flawed." Richard Locke (2013, 67) concludes in his review of years of Nike audits that despite general improvement, the results have been at best "limited, and perhaps, mixed." Upon examining the same factories over time, in almost 80% of Nike suppliers, workplace conditions either remained the same or worsened over time. Noncompliance among Nike suppliers persisted through many years of auditing. In examining a global clothing manufacturer with rigorous audit procedures due to media scrutiny, his team found that only 24% were in full compliance with the company's code of conduct and 53% were explicitly "not approved."

MSIntegrity, a UK-based NGO, finds in a comprehensive report (see references for website, no date, accessed 2021) that multi-stakeholder initiatives are weak. MSI membership is voluntary, thus not all companies are included, which obviously limits the possibilities for changing corporate behavior. Furthermore, NGOs or CSOs lack the capacity or training for auditing and monitoring or necessary deep background in the sectors and become involved in a conflict of interest when they accept corporate contracts to do so. The codes tend to focus on a narrow technocratic scope in reporting, ignoring industry-wide issues. They furthermore ignore the capacity or willingness of host governments in the South to enforce basic standards. Reporting tends to rely on, and push the costs upon, local partners who do not have the capacity, means, or willingness to create comprehensive reports. No effort is made to train local auditors or ensure their independence (Hira et al. 2019). Moreover, there is a lack of enforcement and follow-through, both on the local level and among companies experiencing violations. Finally, there is no real study of impacts.

At this point, *there are no MSIs or company or sectoral (private regime) reporting systems that meet the basic criteria for auditing independence laid out in the introduction*; most would struggle to meet just one or two of them. In fact, the MSIntegrity project finds multiple fatal flaws across the board in the MSIs that include sector-specific MSIs. MSIntegrity underplays perhaps the most problematic factor, of host governments who do not share in the responsibility for reporting or for enforcement of domestic laws, which are frequently ignored on labor and environment. For example, governments do not report how mining revenues are spent if they are part of the EITI or GRI (Hira 2020b), and governments are not required to enforce labor laws even after major scandals such as the Rana Factory collapse in Bangladesh (Hira 2017). We refer readers to MSIntegrity's comprehensive overview to reveal the overall deficiencies (https://www.msi-integrity.org/not-fit-for-purpose/) of MSIs.

Even on the principles for which there is industry consensus, there is no real accountability or enforcement. Boiral et al. (2019) point to flaws in the auditing systems around sustainability reporting, based on interviews with practitioners in the field. First, they note the inherent conflict of interest around companies hiring auditors to verify their compliance. Second, "assurance providers may be tempted to conduct superficial and symbolic rather than substantial verifications." The reporting organizations control the most critical aspects of who does the audit, the scope of the audit, and their access to information. Third, there are basic conflicts among most audit firms who also do consulting work for the same companies. Fourth, there is a limited pool of auditors most of whom are immersed in the same corporate culture and likely enjoy personal ties with companies in the sector, which is why companies select them. Once the company receives a positive audit, it's likely to hire the same firm, thus largely ensuring the same methods and results. Fifth, if a company is in the auditing business, it is in its interests to reduce costs as much as possible and thus avoid undertaking any more complex or less than apparent analysis of factors such as local community social license. Thus, auditing reports are largely superficial and technical, designed for the select audience of company officials to assure investment managers, rather than the array of stakeholders. To provide concrete examples of the flaws in global reporting systems, we present mini case studies of three of the most prominent MSIs.

Case Studies of Global Reporting Regimes: Lots of Reporting, Not Much Accountability

The Global Compact

The UN's Global Compact (https://www.unglobalcompact.org/, accessed June 17, 2021) is a harbinger of the current MSI era. The UN signaled IOs' willingness to work with the corporate sector as an organizer and mediator to bring about the collective good of enforceable and accountable CSR supporting sustainable development. The Compact includes over 12,000 companies in over 160 countries across every sector. The subpage for the Global Compact on its mission leads with the title "Business as a force for good" and provides the ten principles for good behavior around: human rights; labor; environment; and anti-corruption. The Compact offers technical support as well as working with the corporate sector to develop new guidelines. One example of a recent policy initiative is the news item from the webpage "No major G7 stock index aligned with Paris climate goals" which states that none of the companies represented in major Northern countries are meeting climate change emissions reductions goals and calls for them to do so.[1] The Compact delists participating companies, numbering 13,762 as of July 29, 2021, for failure to submit communication on progress reports.[2] There is no way to download the database and sorting is limited to entries on the page, so it is impossible to analyze the data. However, a perusal of several thousand of the firms reveals that they are of diverse geographic origins and small- or medium-sized companies that are unrecognizable as global companies. The UN also decided in 2017 to exclude tobacco companies.

Governance of the Compact is rife with conflicts of interest. The Global Compact's Board, as of June 2021, includes twenty-two members, a Chair, and a Vice-Chair. The Chair is the UN Secretary-General, and the Vice-Chair is a former CEO of Unilever. There are *eleven members from business (50%)*, five members from civil society and labor groups (23%); and six members from Other (27%). The Other category has five members from other IOs and one member of the Danish Foreign Ministry. Financial support comes from governments and business contributions to the Global Compact Foundation. Companies are given guidelines for how much to give based on the size of their annual gross sales/revenues. The 2020 Annual Management

---

1 https://www.unglobalcompact.org/news/4705-06-10-2021, Accessed June 17, 2021.
2 https://www.unglobalcompact.org/participation/report/cop/create-and-submit/expelled?, Accessed July 29, 2021.

Report states that overall revenues for 2020 were $28,548,122, of which governments contributed $3,965,255 (14%), and *companies' required contributions were $10,921,042 (38%)*; the rest was raised from other sources such as events and sponsorships, along with the use of the logo, all of which one must assume is also coming from companies. The same report mentions targets for overall number of companies, and for ones that have over $50 million in annual revenues were met, with 12,388 signed up, well beyond the target of 11,247. The report also notes that the number of integrity issues raised by third parties was twelve in 2020, down from twenty-four in 2019 and eighteen in 2018. One matter triggered a letter of concern from the Compact Executive to the company (32–34) (but nothing more).

Under the integrity sub-page, they mention two key avenues: communication on progress to stakeholders (a reporting function), that includes the ability of companies to use the Global Compact logo, and facilitating dialogue, ones that have no enforcement or accountability power. The 2015 Integrity policy document states that the Compact is willing to take third-party complaints and will ask the company to respond and encourage resolution. After a lengthy appeals process, if the company has not responded to resolve the issue, it may be removed from the Global Compact.

McIntosh et al. (2004) give a very positive early assessment of the Compact, revealing an apologetic explanation of its shortcomings, perhaps not surprising given that Kofi Annan, the former UN Secretary-General, is a co-author. They state that "The Global Compact is not a regulatory instrument-it does not 'police', enforce or measure the behavior or actions of companies. Rather, the Global Compact relies on public accountability, transparency, and the enlightened self-interest of companies, labor, and civil society to initiate and share substantive action in pursuing the principles [...]." (11). They go on to state that the Compact includes all the relevant social actors: governments, companies, CSOs, and the UN (11–12). The overall argument of their volume centers on the idea that regulation is not possible; that the Compact has produced anecdotal evidence of companies changing to conform to its principles; and that it represents an overall "cognitive shift" by companies to accept responsibility for factors beyond the bottom line. Rasche and Waddock (2014) similarly anticipate critics in stating that the Compact's aims were rather modest, that is, to provide a framework to guide corporations who want to be more responsible toward collective action that allows for the slow diffusion of norms transformed into practices. They further point out that a more stringent regulatory system was impossible, as reflected in the slow uptake of the UN Code of Conduct on Transnational Corporations, which was abandoned in 1994, because governments and companies were unwilling to take it up. Thus, the Compact reflects a general shift in strategy from "a reactive strategy trying to police the behavior of businesses toward a more proactive strategy focused on the contributions of firms to development. The agenda moved from confrontation to partnership and collaboration." In other words, the positive reviews are based on making the best of severe limitations in transparency and accountability that are inherent in international organizations' capabilities, not on solving collective action problems of labor and environmental standards.

Most other academic assessments are far more critical of the Compact's performance. Sethi and Schepers (2014) point out that business interests dominate the Board of the Compact and it is beholden to companies financially. They are skeptical about the Compact's claims of progress which rest upon the number of companies who have signed up. They observe that hundreds of companies advertise their membership to the Compact, but say nothing about how they adhere to its principles. They cite the example of PetroChina which was allowed to stay in the Compact despite complaints from civil society about human rights abuses in Sudan. They note that the Compact has a staff of less than thirty to review corporate reporting, thus such efforts have yielded accusations of "bluewashing." They note in regard to enforcement activities, "there is buzzing sound but no discernible message; there is motion, but no direction; and, there is activity, but no measurable impact." They elaborate further in their conclusion:

> A major issue lies in the fact that the UNGC has projected itself as the empyrean of high moral and humanistic values, while in practice, it has struggled in the trenches with lowly mortals, not to save them, but for their patronage to save itself. In this position, the UNGC is incapable of either redeeming itself or making discernible progress in its mission. Perhaps the most honorable approach would be for the UNGC to admit its failure and dissolve itself. Paradoxically, it might even help the UNGC garner more success in changing corporate behavior. When shorn of the UNGC's protective umbrella, corporations will have to respond to public pressure for better conduct, increased responsibility, and verifiable transparency in public disclosure.

Berliner and Prakash (2015) assess the Compact by examining the human rights and environmental performance of 3,000 US firms from 2000 to 2010 using KLD (socially responsible investment, SRI) ratings (see below). They find that members fare worse than non-members. Runhaar and Lafferty (2009) examine in more depth three telecommunications companies to see how signing the Compact affected their behavior. Because the Compact does not provide industry-specific guidance, its impact is at best diffuse.

They could not find any direct evidence of the impact on CSR strategies of the companies (492). Their approach stands in contrast to more correlational or survey approaches that tend to find positive CSR impacts from companies joining the Compact (e.g., Ortas et al. 2015), or negative ones for non-compliance in reporting or being de-listed (Amer 2018), both in the form of studies of differences in share price movements.

In sum, the Compact offers companies a form of advertising their ethical behavior with the UN's stamp of approval in the form of the logo. There is evidence that companies benefit from such reputational brandishing with very limited meaningful enforcement of standards. While one can argue that it has pushed companies to formally adopt certain principles, the lack of any clear monitoring or enforcement system for actual (as opposed to self-reported) behavior (outside of major reported scandals that require only formal reaction by companies) means that the Compact *cannot* point to any major shift in corporate behavior over time. Even if such a shift has happened, which is dubitable, there is no monitoring system to demonstrate it. One has to wonder what is the point of such a system and all the costs involved; more cynically one can see it as a well-meaning system that has been co-opted by companies for branding purposes.

Global Reporting Initiative

The GRI is one of the most extensive sustainability reporting efforts, covering forty-three countries. The GRI came from a project of the Coalition for Environmentally Responsible Economies and the UN Environmental Program, who together created the first reporting guidelines in 2000, inspired by the founding of GRI in 1997 in Boston, in response to the Exxon Valdez oil spill in Alaska. The reporting guidelines center on three basic principles: transparency, inclusiveness, and auditability. Inclusiveness reflects a desire to include stakeholders in the reporting process. Auditability seeks compliance with professional accounting standards (Moneva et al. 2019). GRI states its reporting principles as stakeholder inclusiveness, sustainability context, completeness, and materiality (or inclusion of indicators relevant to stakeholders) (Almeida Machado et al. 2021). GRI offers a database of company reports, including indicators for the level of adherence to GRI standards. Sasse-Werhahn (2019) argues that GRI offers "practical wisdom" in pushing companies to report on material indicators and to engage with stakeholders.

Governance issues parallel those with the Compact; corporations control the GRI and thus there is no effective independence. The GRI website (no date) states that the Secretariat is based in Amsterdam and that there are seven regional hubs. It states that there are over 10,000 GRI reporters in over 100 countries. The organization includes a variety of boards, councils, and working groups in which interested parties can participate, through a nomination and voting process. GRI also invites public comments on proposed updates to standards, which are organized by sector. As the website states, the goal is to "create a common language for organizations—large or small, private or public—to report on their sustainability impacts in a consistent and credible way. This enhances global comparability and enables organizations to be transparent and accountable."

The main body that sets global standards is the Global Sustainability Standards Board. The Board at the time of writing includes a Chair and Vice-Chair, both with consulting backgrounds; two members with labor backgrounds; five representatives from CSR spots in corporations ("business enterprises"); two members from investment institutions; one member of a civil society organization; and two from mediating institutions. *If one considers all of the consulting/business/investment members, therefore, they control nine or fourteen (or 65%) of the votes.* Examining the biographies of the three last members is also instructive. The civil society member has a PhD in environmental science and law and has worked as a consultant. The two members from "mediating institutions" also work as consultants and have strong ties to businesses. While the level of expertise of the members is laudatory, *there does not seem to be representation from civil society or NGOs who might provide a critical angle,* and the voting process is dominated by business interests. The Stakeholder Council is similarly stacked with forty-eight total members, of which twenty-one members are from business and seven from investment institutions; seven members from CSOs and three from labor organizations; and ten members from "mediating institutions," all of whom are consultants. Thus, *59% of votes are controlled by business and investment;* including the "mediating" consultants, this would rise to 79% of votes. *Moreover, GRI notes that 60% of its budget comes from corporations,* and another 40% from governments and foundations.

Parsa et al.'s (2018) study of GRI reports compared to on-the-ground labor and human rights conditions, concludes "Indeed, there appears to be a (deliberate) misinterpretation of the guidelines by TNCs (Transnational Corporations), whereby TNCs easily over-claimed their adherence to the guidelines without being found out or any independent external body flagging out what TNCs did not report and got away with." In short, there is no way to support GRI's claim to be a multi-stakeholder institution; the process is rigged to be controlled by businesses with a stake, essentially reflecting a self-reporting exercise.

The standards themselves are wide-ranging, and though they focus on ESG, they include other items of widespread interest such as incidences of corruption and local procurement spending. The standards call for transparency in terms of taxes paid and for stakeholder engagement. The guide is written in accounting terms, emphasizing accuracy and due diligence in reporting. For example, the standards around materials include amounts of "materials used by weight or volume; recycled input materials used; and reclaimed products and their packaging materials." The guidelines for energy reporting include consumption, intensity, and efforts to reduce energy usage. In terms of governance, there are requirements around reporting on diversity in governance bodies and the ratio of women to men in terms of salary. GR-407 also includes freedom of association and collective bargaining, and GR-408, child labor reporting; GR-411, violations of rights of indigenous peoples. This huge laundry list of exclusively quantitative indicators must present quite a burden to reporting units in the companies. While certainly having value, as in all IOs, *any qualitative assessment of politics or reporting of conflict or tension is assiduously avoided.* Simply reporting potential violations, in short, tells us nothing about the quality of local relations at the corporate site. There is *no requirement for reporting stakeholder views or outcomes in terms of local benefits.* More importantly, there is *no requirement for governments to report on anything, including how they use the revenues they receive from companies* (Hira 2020a). Each GRI standard includes the legal liability statement:

> While the GRI Board of Directors and GSSB encourage use of the GRI Sustainability Reporting Standards (GRI Standards) and related Interpretations by all organizations, the preparation and publication of reports based fully or partially on the GRI Standards and related Interpretations are the full responsibility of those producing them. Neither the GRI Board of Directors, GSSB nor Stichting Global Reporting Initiative (GRI) can assume responsibility for any consequences or damages resulting directly or indirectly from the use of the GRI Standards and related Interpretations in the preparation of reports, or the use of reports based on the GRI Standards and related Interpretations.

This reflects the fact, as reported by several authors (e.g., Barkemeyer et al. 2015; Bilbao-Terol et al. 2018), that *many companies are not in compliance with GRI reporting standards and that there is a general inconsistency across reporting.* Moreover, there is no clarity or consistency for stakeholder engagement, a supposedly vital input to reporting (Almeida Machado 2021). In other words, there is no real accountability in GRI standards. Indeed, there does not appear to be any grading or auditing, or enforcement mechanism on the website. *Nor is there any evidence that the GRI reporting has any connection to real outcomes.* For example, Belkhir et al. (2017) compare forty A-grade GRI reporting companies with twenty-four non-reporting companies in terms of CO_2 emissions, controlling for sector, and find no differences.

Boiral (2013) uses the term "simulacrum" coined by the French philosopher Baudrillard, meaning a phenomenon that is completely artificial and divorced from reality, but perceived as real, to describe what he finds in the GRI reporting system. He examined twenty-three A- and A+-rated companies in the GRI system in terms of company reports and did a content analysis of news stories about them to check for possible violations of sustainability practices. He found over 116 separate events that were nowhere reflected in company reports. In fact, the reports were overwhelmingly positive and did not reflect any of the challenges one would expect in everyday business, such as differing views of stakeholders. Lozano (2013) notes that there is little to no attempt in most company reports to link indicators across E, S, and G together to evaluate whether sustainable development has been achieved. Boiral and Henri (2015), after examining twelve GRI sustainability reports from mining companies, conclude that performance is ultimately subjective, citing a lack of qualitative discussion; lack of compliance with GRI protocols; ambiguous or incomplete or inconsistent data, information, and indicators, all leading to overall report opacity. This reflects an overall subjectivity of both the reports and how reporting managers consider sustainability.

In regard to the requirements for stakeholder reporting, Joseph (2012) states, "The absence of norms and criteria for identifying stakes of such 'dependent' stakeholders, limits the extent to which firms will disclose such stakes or specifically address the 'reasonable expectations' of such stakeholders." By dependent stakeholders, they refer to groups such as local civil society who typically lack any real power to have their voice heard. Therefore, "GRI extends the traditional accounting lens into the stakeholder theory, though the view is now murky, with more latitude and an onus on the development of measures, without seriously examining areas of ambiguities or the necessity for sustainability to provide firms a new vision of their role in society. Sustainable development or the goal of inter-generational equity is open to interpretation, and the relationship of such a goal to that of the firm is not addressed." To sum up, *while stakeholder engagement is a fundamental criterion for accountability, stakeholders have no ability to report information.* The end result of GRI is another empty exercise.

Extractive Industries Transparency Initiative

The EITI is widely considered the leading index for mineral resources, including the oil and gas sectors. It began in 2003 during a meeting of governments, industries, and civil society groups who agreed on "EITI Principles," and the organization was founded in 2006 as a non-profit in Norway (Sovacool and Andrews 2015). As with other CSR indices, David-Barret and Okamura (2016) theorize EITI as a form of norm diffusion by Western governments seeking reassurance for their investors and consumers. Thus, the EITI label offers the potential for increased investment through improving the reputation of the target country. In fact, they find EITI membership confers increased aid and debt forgiveness, thus supporting their contention of normative change for improved resources.

Governance issues of the EITI parallel those of our other mini-cases. The EITI website states that their mission is "to promote understanding of natural resource management, strengthen public and corporate governance and provide the data to inform greater transparency and accountability in the extractives sector" since a country's natural resources "belong to its citizens." They further state, "By becoming a member of the EITI, countries commit to disclose information along the extractive industry value chain— from how extraction rights are awarded, to how revenues make their way through the government and how they benefit the public." EITI requires a multi-stakeholder group of government, civil society, and companies in each country to meet. It also has reporting requirements for companies around payments to governments that are made publicly available. EITI offers a candidacy period for countries wishing to join to meet standards and periodic reviews. The overall organization is managed by the EITI Board. The Board for 2019–22 includes a Chair, who is a former New Zealand politician; twelve members from implementing countries; four members from supporting countries (Canada, the Netherlands, France, and Belgium); ten members from CSOs (civil society organizations); twelve members from companies, including investors; and the Executive Director of the Secretariat. In sum, there are *seventeen members from the government (43%) and twelve members from companies (31%); leaving civil society with just 25% of the votes.* In a recurring pattern, we see that CSOs are again in a minority position, and must acknowledge that coming from different countries their ability to act as a collective force is considerably more challenging than governments and companies who are pro-investment and benefit directly from it.

The conflicts of interest run deeper than just representation on the board. EITI relied in 2020 on *governments for 60% ($4.524 million) of its financial contributions, on the private sector for another 30% ($1.977 million),* and on implementing countries for another 10% ($67,000) according to the 2021 Progress Report from its website. Klein (2017) estimates $50 million annually is spent on EITI activities by the Secretariat and countries. She points to notable improvements in disclosures and a more vigorous role for civil society, though the latter struggle to understand the technical reports. Still, one has to question again the potential for neutrality when government and the private sector are paying for the salaries and costs of the Secretariat.

Clearly, companies providing close to $2 million annually will expect to have a strong voice in governance; CSOs, by contrast, will be underfunded in their efforts to provide information.

Violations are cited and remediation is required for continuing in good status. EITI gives three main areas of assessment: stakeholder engagement; transparency; and outcomes and impact. Validations scores are given on a 100-point scale and color-coded under red (not met, 0) to yellow (partly met, 30) to blue and green (60 and above). The website does not indicate how data are translated into scores, and the website does not give any specific consequences for failing to meet violations, stating "Countries are expected to keep improving their score from one Validation to the next, but will not be sanctioned for not meeting all EITI Requirements within a certain timeframe. Where improvements are made between Validations, but do not result in a change in the category of progress, countries may be awarded additional points to reflect progress towards meeting the Requirement concerned."[3] There is a timeframe of up to twenty-four months for "corrective actions." Furthermore, *the EITI Secretariat itself makes the assessments; there is no independent verification.*

Sovacool (2020) finds strong positive correlations between EITI status and The World Bank's transparency indicators, however, these are mostly in the economic arena (as reflected in EITI's focus on revenue reporting). He paints EITI as a necessary and positive ingredient in improved governance. Similarly, Vijge (2018) concludes that the introduction of EITI in Myanmar gave CSOs a new level of recognition. However, he notes "Though the EITI in Myanmar has empowered certain CSOs to demand accountability of the government and companies regarding the adverse impacts of extractive industries, CSOs' ability to *evoke* response and action from responsible actors is limited, mainly because of institutional constraints." Riter's (2019) review of EITI concludes that it is an important step in getting corporations to accept some responsibility for transparency and governance.

While the accountability and enforcement mechanisms are theoretically improved over GRI, there are still major issues.

- First, there is a lack of clear transparency and traceability to how validations scores or remedial progress are measured.
- Second, there is clearly a conflict of interest in that governments are assessing other governments, and companies other companies. There is no independent oversight.

---

3 https://eiti.org/news/new-approach-to-assessing-progress-in-eiti-countries, Accessed June 14, 2021.

- Third, the civil society roundtable can make comments, which is helpful, but has no ability to do anything beyond that.
- Finally, there are to be lax standards or consequences for violations.

In examining the 100 validation decisions given on the EITI website, only two listed inadequate progress. All the rest state "meaningful" or "satisfactory" progress had been achieved.[4] One has to wonder, then, why EITI is needed when there is by and large full compliance.

EITI does appear to have improved the reporting of payments by companies to governments. However, *there is no requirement in reporting of resource expenditures by governments* (Requirement 5.1). They merely need to discuss how much money they collected, not how they spent the funds. Thus, the EITI system *does little to wipe out systematic corruption.* For example, *Nigeria* is a member of EITI, and *won an EITI award in 2013* (Zalik and Osuaka 2020), though it ranks 149th in terms of the 2020 Transparency International Corruption Perceptions Index. Nigeria's corruption score is 25, which puts it in the range of highly corrupt. Another member, the Democratic Republic of the Congo, ranks 170th and has a score of 18, ranking it even more highly corrupt. These are just two examples of several highly corrupt countries with EITI endorsement.[5] Furthermore, there is no requirement for spending mining revenues on items that will help local communities or lead to measurable development outcomes. So, all we have are the amounts paid by companies to governments, which has nothing to do with how that money was spent, or whether it went to corruption rather than concrete outcomes for the countries providing the minerals.

The likely response to EITI and others to such critiques is that the effort is too shallow to capture all the benefits of its reporting including indirect pressures for responsible behavior through the pledges taken by the parties toward greater transparency. We would simply respond that *pledges mean nothing if there is no responsibility to uphold them.* Moreover, our conclusion here is in consonance with other analyses. The MSIntegrity report reflects several years of reporting on CSR by a large international research group, including in-person witnessing of how international accountability agencies conduct business. Their analysis of EITI is troubling. They point out that "it is not uncommon" for EITI and similar initiatives to make remedial suggestions that are discussed and revised for years, but action is never taken (78–79). They review the structural flaws for civil society organization members seeking to participate in EITI as a reporting entity,

---

4 https://eiti.org/validation-decisions-schedule, Accessed June 14, 2021.
5 https://www.transparency.org/en/cpi/2020/index/nzl, Accessed June 14, 2021.

with no consequence: heavy and complex workload, including the challenges of translating their often contentious home constituencies into the technical language of EITI or the resources/expertise to grapple with complex financial reporting; they represent a minority on the twenty-one-person EITI Board, as noted above; and it is extremely challenging for them to organize an overall global civil society agenda to present to the EITI Board, whereas governments and companies are much more aligned, resourced, and capable. Thus decision-making processes are subject to " 'corporate capture', in which corporations exercise undue influence over these initiatives while excluding CSOs and rights holders from equal opportunities to effect change" (83). They further point out that EITI does not allow anonymous complaints or publish received complaints, thus shutting off potentially important sources of information (169, 178). Finally, they note that there is no attempt to measure impact assessment on EITI, which instead relies on macro indicators such as poverty reduction, economic growth, and investment climate. Thus, there is no proximate indicator of transparency or governance (203).

The sources of information that EITI relies upon for its self-evaluation are particularly important. The sources are all general indices of governance, such as those from the World Bank, Freedom House, and the World Economic Forum (EITI 2021). There is *no attempt to gather on-the-ground data*, and this must explain why EITI is so out of touch with the reality of continued poverty and frustration in local communities. An independent evaluation of EITI based on stakeholder interviews concludes (Scanteam 2011, iv).

> The lack of societal results is confirmed by testing "Big picture" indicators proposed by EITI. This revealed that there is not any solid theory of change behind some of the EITI aspirations, nor do data show any links at this aggregate level. Results focus should therefore rather be at country level. But the lack of societal change is also a function of the narrow focus of EITI activities.

Scanteam further notes that "while *transparency* has improved, *accountability* does not appear to have changed much, in part because necessary political, legal and institutional improvements have in most cases not been put in place (3)." They further note that while societal actors have been engaged, they have not been empowered. They also highlight the lack of consideration of country context (32–33).

By contrast, a 2016 GIZ (German aid agency) report is quite positive about the relevance and importance of EITI for promoting transparency around revenue management including its reporting process. However, they also conclude that transparency is not linked to accountability, that EITI lacks a theory of change, and that it does not have an adequate monitoring and evaluation system. They particularly recommend including the perception of local stakeholders in such a system, and for qualitative evidence to be included (10–12). As noted above, this author complained about the lack of transparency indicated by civil society groups around mining and verified through six weeks of field research in a Latin American country including an extensive in-depth household survey in the mining community conducted by a highly reputable local partner. After relaying deep community concerns to the EITI, the EITI's initial response was that it could not consider the information, since its reporting cycle and admission of the country to good candidate status had just taken place. It promised to take it into account in the next cycle, however, despite multiple notes from the author, the country was given a positive review in the next cycle, without addressing any of the blatant lack of transparency around mining revenues, and civil society protests related to them. In other words, the EITI chose to ignore egregious violations of its own principles, not even bothering to investigate the complaints brought by its own civil society group. One has to ask what the point of such principles is, beyond corporate and host government greenwashing.

The literature backs up such conclusions. For example, in regard to environmental reporting under EITI, Rita Sequeira et al. (2016) find in Zambia that EITI reporting requirements make little difference in how companies report and are not transparent or useful enough for civil society to verify government or company claims. Hoinathy and Jánsky's (2017) review of the effects of EITI membership on Chad's governance is remarkably consonant with the aforementioned studies. There was an increase in information disclosure, however, the information was limited and so technical that only a small group of co-opted civil society "transparency experts" could participate in the EITI roundtables. Nothing changed in terms of the overall corruption or outcomes of the mineral sector.

Furthermore, Ejiogu et al. (2019)'s portrait of how EITI operates in Nigeria is hardly reassuring. In their dark conclusion, EITI indicators are opaque and largely "unintelligible" to civil society; controlled by the EITI which they view as a corrupt and elite agency, politicized by the government; and that the net effect is "distrust, uncertainty, and doubt" among readers of its reports. Öge's (2016) study of Azerbaijan (which subsequently left the EITI) and Kazakhstan reaches parallel conclusions of technocratic language and effective co-optation of civil society groups by the state. With limited access to funding, limited technical capacity, and in the midst of general political repression, civil society advocates have limited ability to take advantage of the voice option EITI affords. These findings are reinforced by Sovacool and Andrews' (2015) study of Azerbaijan and Liberia, where in both cases EITI became co-opted by government and company forces, reflecting the weakness of civil society groups. In these cases, EITI did nothing to improve overall governance. They add the following important point, "the EITI tries to ensure that the revenues from their extraction become more accountable, but it does not ensure that they become more socially and environmentally sustainable." In short, there are major costs to any type of resource extraction, and the issues go far beyond lack of transparency.

On the broad question about whether the EITI is achieving its overall mission, López-Cazar et al. (2021) examine five Latin American countries to see if EITI membership had any effect on corruption levels; they find no such relationship. In fact, in some cases, corruption worsened after membership. Bebbington et al. (2017) take a more nuanced approach to EITI adoption in the Andes, arguing that the effectiveness, shape, and parameters were driven largely by domestic political factors. They see EITI playing a positive role in opening up civil society space, but *only where* the politics and processes were already moving in that direction.

Furstenberg (2018) describes a troubling situation around EITI in Kazakhstan, where EITI was adopted amidst worker and popular protests amidst corruption allegations in the oil and gas sectors. Beyond superficial indicators, there is little information about company expenditures, and there is no transparency in regard to state decisions on revenues. Nor is the state required to disclose the terms of its contracts with private companies. The EITI civil society roundtable membership is rigged and cowed by state and company actors and lacks the capacity to understand technical issues. Moreover, there is still an atmosphere of repression that prevents frank speech. The end result is that, far from separating the ruling family dynasty from the resource sector, it further ensconced it through more formal institutional channels. Oppong and Andrews (2020) paint a more complex picture of how EITI has played out in Ghana's oil industry. While opening the way for greater civil society knowledge of the oil sector, the authors argue that the entire process, including auditing, has been subject to elite control, and thus is fundamentally a "technocratic" exercise.

So, why does EITI persist at an annual cost of millions in reporting time and funding support when its results are so limited? The answer is simple— it provides a veneer of legitimacy for investment in mining operations. As Malden (2017) and Öge (2016) find, EITI has a positive effect on mineral investment. Not surprisingly given our review of the literature, Corrigan's (2017) econometric model finds that EITI membership is associated with higher levels of GDP per capita, but there is no effect on levels of corruption; this is confirmed by Kasekende et al. (2016) who find EITI membership is actually associated with increased corruption. Nor should it be surprising that countries that are more self-sufficient in terms of mineral investment and extraction capacity, such as Saudi Arabia, Russia, and Iran, are not members of EITI. As Kasekende et al. (2016) point out, only partial revenue information is disclosed, leaving many aspects of contracts opaque. Moreover, audit recommendations "are blatantly ignored despite serious irregularities." Perhaps the weakest part of EITI is that it focuses only on transparency in revenues and does nothing with expenditures.

As reflected in our examination of the Compact and the GRI, the EITI is essentially a technocratic marketing exercise that ignores most of the factors that lead to resource conflict: including ethnic/political tensions; patronage, corruption, and weak accountability in government institutions; the lack of concern for local communities who are marginalized from the benefits of resources taken from their area; the lack of local capacity to enter into supply chains and mining itself; and the lack of a prudent macroeconomic framework to manage the resource curse through booms and busts.

Conclusion: Global CSR Reporting Is Self-Reporting

As we have seen, global CSR reporting systems set up to assure consumers, investors, and Western governments of the propriety of Western companies do little to address the fundamental causes of corruption and misuse of resource revenues in reality. It may be pictured as a tentative first step, but given the huge reporting hurdles and funds invested, it is hard to tie GRI or EITI to actual outcomes or tangible improvements for civil society and equitable and sustainable development. The author has seen this on the ground at mining sites in the global South, where companies who won global CSR awards were viewed by 90+% of the population as contributing little to development. Many of the award winning communities remain locked in abject poverty, with little to show for the mining or labor assembly operations.

In short, CSR reporting systems lack transparency, accountability, and enforcement. They are essentially self-reporting exercises, with companies dominating all key decisions. *No company would approach its business operations or contracts with such shoddy oversight.* Surely such vast expenditures on the MSIs could be better invested into more concrete results for the pressing development needs of civil society in the South. Yet, as long as companies continue to see a benefit to such superficial exercises, and IOs and NGOs continue to give their blessings, nothing will change.

Almost all NGOs are constantly raising funds, and operate with heavy staff turnover and a largely volunteer and temporary workforce, reducing their potential effectiveness as professional organizations. Many colleagues have argued that most NGOs are sound, and that "everyone knows" which ones are true and which are co-opted. However, it's clear that they fundamentally suffer from the same accountability issues as corporations, beyond the fact that they are not professionally trained in auditing. Just think of recent scandals around once renowned NGOs, such as the Red Cross, Oxfam, and the WE Charity, with the first and last linked to the inability to account for millions in donations, and the second to sexual exploitation. Similar scandals have wracked IOs including the UN and IOs constantly seeking new funding have found CSR reporting a ready source.[6] *How can unaccountable NGOs and IOs provide accountability?* Thus, *CSR is more properly seen as motivated by collective action toward establishing a perception of good corporate behavior.* Marketing the perception, in short, is far cheaper than engaging in the costly tasks of cutting off fossil fuels or avoiding the use of child or sweatshop labor or genuinely improving living standards in marginalized communities. Even in the face of such deficiencies, the generally oblivious Western consumer will not be the wiser, seeing ethical labeling and CSR self-reporting as a form of blissful reassurance. Media attention is focused on one-off events such as factory collapses, rather than the everyday grind of labor exploitation and environmental degradation. Unless there is a shift towards genuine transparency and accountability, in short, companies are incentivized to cheat.

As opposed to the billions of (largely) blissfully ignorant, unaware, and disorganized consumers, SRI is far more concentrated and expert-oriented as it depends on the decisions of professional money managers who are supposed to reflect the values of their clients. Unlike the episodic nature of activism based on scandals, SRI wields true and consistent power in the form of investment decisions. Money managers guide the vast pools of capital and are able to research company behavior in response to their investors' needs. The most important ones are the pension funds representing often progressive public sector unions and reflect a highly visible and tangible, market-moving presence by their sheer size. It seems highly dubitable that SRI managers can be co-opted by companies so easily as fund-starved IOs or NGOs; they, and not companies, should be in the driver's seat by virtue of the capital they control and its mobility. Beyond the global MSI reporting vehicles, there is thus a whole new industry of ESG reporting designed specifically for these activist shareholders. We now turn to assessing private sector ESG ratings systems that inform the vast pools of capital controlled by institutional investors.

---

6 https://www.npr.org/2015/06/03/411524156/in-search-of-the-red-cross-500-million-in-haiti-relief; https://www.bbc.com/news/health-56670162; https://www.cbc.ca/news/canada/we-charity-misled-donors-records-show-1.6251985; https://www.theguardian.com/tv-and-radio/2018/aug/01/the-un-sex-abuse-scandal-tv-review, https://www.devex.com/news/devexplains-an-inside-look-at-the-unops-scandal-103265; All accessed December 9, 2021.

Chapter 3

SOCIALLY RESPONSIBLE INVESTMENT REPORTING: A LUCRATIVE AND GROWING BUSINESS

Introduction

Since the 1990s, a revolution in global finance has taken place, namely the rise of socially responsible investment (SRI) that pushes for corporate social responsibility (CSR). SRI seeks to take ethically responsible positions in regard to social, labor, governance, and environmental issues, often summarized as ESG, for environmental, social, and governance criteria. SRI gained momentum from religious movements opposing the Vietnam War and apartheid in South Africa (Knoll 2002, 684–85). Boffo and Patalano (2020, 6) estimate the SRI market to be worth at least $17.5 trillion. A 2018 article by Mellow offers an even higher estimate of at least $23 trillion of investment capital in socially responsible funds, and that at least 61% of institutional investors integrate environmental, social, and governance (ESG) factors into their fundamental decision-making process. SRI is concentrated among large institutional investors, such as pension funds and universities (Scholtens and Sievänen 2013). SRI can take the form of shareholder activism, that is, making demands on companies for ethical behavior, or through "negative screening," that is, declining to invest in companies that are viewed as unethical. In some cases, SRI investors choose to place money into community-based institutions, such as local credit banks. Large public or religious private institutions such as universities, labor unions, or churches face pressure from students and faculty/workers and board members to make ethical investment decisions.

Bebchuk and Hirst (2019) underline just how concentrated capital investment has become, thus underscoring the importance of the reports they rely upon. In the United States, the "Big Three" index fund managers of Blackrock, Vanguard, and State Street Global Advisors dominate capital markets. More than 80% of all investment fund assets come through them, with the proportion rising over time; their combined stake in S&P companies rose from 5% in 1998 to 21% in 2017; these three funds now hold 5% or more of the shares of most companies in the S&P 500, with an average combined stake of over 30%; and they control an average of about 25% of all shares in director elections in the S&P 500. Thus, decision-making on the part of this handful of institutional investors can effectively move markets.

Institutional investors represent 84% of UK total shareholdings and 61% of those in the United States. In the United States, they manage 80% of share trades. SRI was estimated to value over $2 trillion in the United States and Europe, respectively, in 2008 (Sandberg et al. 2009). Estimates from 2011 put SRI at roughly 11% of professionally managed assets in the United States and 17% in the European Union (EU) (Cortez et al. 2012). Their decisions rest on rating services, such as Bloomberg. Over time, requirements for ethical disclosure of choices by pension funds have come to be a part of financial regulations throughout the West (Renneboog et al. 2008). Amel-Zadeh and Serafeim's (2018) global survey of institutional investors found that 82% of respondents state that they use ESG information because they believe that it affects investment performance. About a third (33%) are motivated by growing client/stakeholder demand. Another 32% are motivated by the belief that it can change corporate behavior to improve ESG outcomes and that it is an ethical responsibility.

As with CSR more generally, there is a great deal of ambiguity around the motivations of institutional investors. There are no clear indications that large numbers of individual investors are willing to make investment decisions on the basis of social responsibility if it trumps return on investment (ROI). Some survey-based research claims that "warm feelings" and peer pressure à la corporate isomorphism are factors that explain SRI's growth (Gutsche et al. 2019). Richardson (2013) offers three alternative perspectives on why SRI exists: "the complicity doctrine, leverage-based responsibility, and the universal owner (UO) thesis." Complicity refers to "negative screening" or excluding "problematic companies" from investment portfolios. This would include avoiding companies who have been accused of human rights violations, corruption, or major environmental disasters. In terms of leverage-based responsibility, the idea is that SRI can be used to improve conditions through using investment to pressure corporations. Here the sanctions against South Africa related to apartheid are the foremost example. However, Richardson points out that the extent of leverage varies and is generally quite limited as capital is almost always pooled through markets. In practice, most financial institutions "would balk" at the idea of applying leverage. Richardson claims the UO is the most prevalent justification for SRI. UO suggests that the largest investors effectively own the economy, and thus have

SOCIALLY RESPONSIBLE INVESTMENT REPORTING   53

responsibility for general, including social and environmental, conditions of the economy that will, in the long run, affect the investment climate and so their potential returns, reflecting a stakeholder approach as described in the last chapter. Richardson notes that the large pension funds CalPERS (representing California public employees) and TIAA-CREF (representing employees in higher education institutions) both employ UO language in describing their ethical decision-making. Yet, definitions of responsible UO are ambiguous and it's hard to trace causal effects. It remains unclear how the investor can link general economic concerns to specific decisions in any systematic way, with the slow response to climate change being a perfect example. Perhaps equally important is the fact that most money managers do not have data around a long-term time horizon of decades to see if general economic and social conditions are improving. Decisions need to be made, with at most a ten-year outlook, but generally in the much more immediate term of 1-5 years. Moreover, investors are driven by market prices, which change on an hourly basis in response to corporate performance and unpredictable economic and political events.

Nonetheless, SRI is gaining increasing attention across the financial and corporate worlds, driven by the ethical inclinations of public sector unions' pension funds and the scrutiny around sovereign wealth funds, who together are "market movers" in terms of their control of vast amounts of capital. There are a number of emerging investment groups such as universities that are seeking new ways to monitor and potentially divest from stocks and funds that are considered unethical. One of the most prominent is the Interfaith Center on Corporate Responsibility, which was set up in 1971 by US religious groups to pressure corporations on CSR; the catalyst was South African apartheid. Their website suggests that they represent over 300 global institutional investors with more than $4 trillion in managed assets (https://www.iccr.org/). In June 2021, they filed a lawsuit in the United States regarding shareholder rights to request company disclosures around CSR concerns. The European Financial Reporting Advisory Group is a highly active private sector group that offers a space for conversations around harmonizing sustainability standards (https://www.efrag.org/).

The Principles for Responsible Investment (PRI), a UN-based agreement, reflects the largest formal core commitment of companies toward ESG principles and is a guiding document for SRI managers. The webpage (https://www.unpri.org/pri/what-are-the-principles-for-responsible-investment, accessed June 16, 2021) states that PRI was developed by a group of international investors, for investors, in order to "contribute to developing a more sustainable global financial system." The PRI secretariat offers resources to signatories, including guidance and case studies. In exchange, signatories must file an annual report. As of June 2021, there were 3,038 signatories. There are twelve board members and a Chair. Reflecting the business orientation of the CSR assurance bodies discussed in the last chapter, seven of twelve (58%) are asset owners; another three are non-asset owners, these appear to include two members from the financial sector and another member from Sustainalytics, a ratings firm (see below), and two permanent members of the UN. There are no members from NGOs or civil society. Access to reports was denied to the author, even after signing up and receiving a clearance (acceptable user) e-mail.[1] It appears data are only available to signatories or their authorized agents. In short, PRI bears the similar conflicts of interest and weaknesses we have seen with Global Reporting Initiative (GRI) and Extractives Industries Transparency Initiative.

There is some cause for optimism. Concerns about the overall detrimental economic impact of climate change are perhaps the greatest catalyst. The Financial Stability Board, an international body for coordinating financial authorities across nations, spun off a Task Force for Climate-Related Disclosures in 2015. The task force appears to be designed to place pressure on companies to reveal their financial positions/assets in carbon-based activities. Disclosing such assets is expected to indirectly pressure companies to start to divest themselves of them. The initiative also stems from the idea that climate change is a systemic risk, alluding to the housing bubble risks leading up to the 2008 crisis. In general, the effort seeks to incorporate what economists call "externalities," costs not borne directly by companies, such as pollution or the detrimental effects of child labor, but which will have a serious detrimental effect on the economic environment over the long term. The Task Force has thirty-two members from the G20 countries, including representatives from large multinationals such as Dow and investment houses such as BlackRock; the Canadian Pension Plan; and J.P. Morgan. The Chair of the Principles for Responsible Investment Group, discussed below, is also a member. The Chair of the Task Force is Michael Bloomberg, whose financial information services company is one of the largest in the world (https://www.fsb-tcfd.org/, accessed July 26, 2021). Large corporate backers support the initiative, including Bank of America, Citigroup, Royal Dutch

---

1 The webpage after signing in stated, "ACCESS NOT AUTHORIZED. Please be advised that if you are a consultant or other external user, not within the signatory organization, then we require someone in the signatory organization to support@unpri.org. Access to the Data Portal will not be provided to a consultant or other external user of a signatory organization, except in the case of a fiduciary manager or a parent/sister organization with the written consent of the organization's main contact." June 16, 2021.

Shell, Iberdrola, and BHP Billiton, as well as large pension funds from around the world, including the Netherlands, Canada, and California. However, major oil companies including BP, Chevron, ConocoPhillips, and Total have demurred (Bifera 2017). Bloomberg is also a champion behind the Sustainability Accounting Standards Board (SASB), which seeks to make non-financial indicators, such as greenhouse gas emissions and labor practices, standard parts of company reporting. They offer a list of suggested standards by industry, which they claim are harmonious with GRI (https://www.sasb.org/about/sasb-and-other-esg-frameworks/; https://materiality.sasb.org/, accessed July 26, 2021). The SASB is backed by some of the largest investment and pension funds that support its work, including BlackRock, Vanguard, and Fidelity (Finley 2020). Perhaps it is not surprising that reporting standards are a growing part of Bloomberg's financial analysis services, as we report below.

The EU is also promoting harmonization of ESG reporting standards beyond the aforementioned efforts of the aforementioned Task Force for Climate-Related Disclosures. The EU, as part of its Green Deal efforts, has been pushing the principle of sustainable finance. In 2020, the EU created a Taxonomy Regulation that classifies business activities in terms of their environmental sustainability. The Non-Financial Reporting Directive requires disclosures by industrial companies, in an effort to assist investors interested in levels of sustainability. Furthermore, the 2021 Financial Services Sustainability Disclosure Requirement introduces a new set of rules around the sustainability of funds and financial products. The European Banking Association also has been discussing a green asset ratio disclosure that would include information about financial institutions' sustainability plans (Bruno and Lagasio 2021). EU efforts include a technical expert group on sustainable finance, whose mandate is to develop a "unified classification system" for sustainable economic activities, and metrics for climate-related disclosures. If harmonized with the SEC disclosure initiatives and combined with a proposed carbon border tax measure, it would give real momentum for developing more meaningful emissions disclosure reporting.[2] While the strategic goals are wide-sweeping, there are still gaps, including the lack of a central supervisor for compliance and no harmonization of liability law or sanctions, thus bringing into question enforcement capacity (Busch 2021). More importantly, there is no indication that the adoption of new sustainability standards will avoid the transparency and accountability issues of the existing CSR reporting systems discussed in Chapter 2.

---

2 https://finance.ec.europa.eu/sustainable-finance/disclosures/eu-labels-benchmarks-climate-esg-and-benchmarks-esg-disclosures_en, Accessed December 15, 2022.

Evaluating the SRI Indices: Literature Review

Money managers for investment firms and pension funds use a growing number of SRI indices provided by business information firms such as Bloomberg to make ethical choices. Yet, there are many reasons to question how much money managers who make decisions *really know* about the ethics of the businesses they are investing in, let alone the nature of the CSR issues that companies face or how to resolve them. Friede et al. (2015) suggest that less than a quarter of investment professionals consider extra-financial information, and only about 10% receive formal training about how to consider ESG criteria in their investment analyses. Similarly, in Amel-Zadeh and Serafeim's 2018 global survey of investment managers, only 8% considered themselves ESG specialists. In fact, data quality and comparability issues as discussed in the section on GRI above are rife throughout ESG reporting, according to an Organisation for Economic Co-operation and Development (OECD) study (Boffo and Patalano 2020). Nielsen and Noergaard's (2011) examination of investor decisions regarding how to consider ESG ratings when making decisions reveals that they are inevitably secondary to ROI. That is, ESG are *only important when they affect profit*; there is no attempt to integrate ESG and ROI as separate streams of data for investment decision-making. The implication is clear—money managers want ready to use screens to avoid scandals, not to make more socially responsible investment decisions.

Boiral et al. (2020) state that the aim of sustainability ratings agencies (SRAs) is to provide a ready-to-use indicator for investment managers' needs to make quick decisions about companies:

> To meet these needs, particularly in terms of rigor and risk measurement, SRAs must quantify elements that seem a priori unmeasurable, uncertain, and elusive (e.g., points of view of certain stakeholders, rumors, press articles, suspicions of misconduct, and allegations of security problems). This quantification process makes it possible to give an objective, measurable, concrete, and manageable appearance to risks that initially seem uncertain and diffuse.

Boiral et al. (2020)'s thirty interviews with SRA analysts reveal a clear pattern of reliance on shorthand assessment devices. There is a tendency to focus on negative screening and "best-in-class" approaches. While some do reach out to NGOs, employees, and other stakeholders who know companies, none of this information is systematically incorporated into ratings. They struggle with attempting to "quantify elements that seem a priori unmeasurable, uncertain, and elusive," such as when stakeholders have different perspectives, or in the case of rumors of scandalous behavior, much of which ratings agencies keep confidential. Thus, 69% of respondents stated that sustainability risk assessment depends on unreliable information. Another 56% of the respondents note the challenges of predicting risks and scandals for companies that are highly rated, such as Volkswagen's scandal around false diesel emission standards. The same proportion acknowledges that "the methods used by agencies appear to be poorly standardized, constantly evolving, and based on often difficult trade-offs," thus comparability across ratings and time and space is impossible. Nor is there any clarity or consistency for how long a company should be penalized for a found violation.

Diouf and Boiral (2017) conducted a similar exercise with thirty-three SRI professionals in Canada. While the respondents felt that GRI reporting added value, they also acknowledge a series of issues that undermine it. First, they acknowledged that only positive items tend to be reported; 90% stated that companies do not publish negative information. Another 70% do not find reporting data to be comparable across companies and 65% found incomparability in individual company reports over time. Similarly, 80% found that GRI reports lack clarity, with basic questions sometimes obscured by detailed but irrelevant information reported. Another 70% have concerns about the assurance/auditing processes to ensure accurate information. In short, ratings efforts generally ignore context and complexity.

Screening is the most basic step for ESG. It involves "negative" screening, which would be eliminating companies deemed by the client to be unethical, such as companies involved in the sale of weapons, alcohol, or pornography. It can also include "positive" screening, which, while more unusual, would mean including companies that have ethical practices, such as company efforts to expand diversity on corporate boards. These appear to be sound starting points. Wagemans et al. (2013) note, however, that screening is a highly problematic process, with arbitrary criteria, and varying methodologies. They provide the example of an organic (natural foods) company with discriminatory hiring being acceptable in some indices. Indeed, Chatterji et al. (2016) find striking divergences among different SRI ratings agencies in the ranking of corporations. Capelle-Blancard and Monjon (2014) take the unusual step of examining the quality of screening information, particularly the diversity and independence of information, financial and CSR expertise, control, reporting, etc. They are unable to reach any clear conclusions about whether the quality of screening information affects financial performance and thus call for more research.

Even a ratings company-sponsored report, SustainAbility (2020, 13–15), notes that: ESG ratings are used differently across different investment/asset management firms; many use multiple ratings firms; and ESG are but one of many different sources of input about company performance, with ratings mainly used to screen out very poorly rated firms. Overall, investors look more closely at business models, and find the ESG ratings full of issues, "from inaccuracies and use of old or backward-looking data, to more fundamental concerns about whether ESG performance can ever be distilled into a single score. Investors also complained about holes in corporate data and the need for companies to improve disclosure, reporting and transparency" (14). Nonetheless, most investment managers effectively use ESG ratings as a *de rigeur* reliable methodology.

There are further issues in terms of consistency and quality of available information from SRI indices and company reporting. For example, Amel-Zadeh and Serafeim (2018) find that there are a number of impediments cited by managers to integrating ESG reporting into decision-making: 45% mentioned a lack of comparability across firms; 43%, the lack of reporting standards; 39% that it is too general to be useful; 38% that it is not quantifiable; and 35% that it is not comparable over time. Avetisyan and Hockerts (2017) note an overall trend toward consolidation of ratings agencies because so many struggle to make ends meet financially. They find less attention to the quality of data and depth of knowledge after mergers and acquisitions of ratings firms. Escrig-Olmedo et al. (2019) furthermore point to the challenges for evaluating ESG indices for SRI that are evolving over time. As they note, most indices do not provide transparency about their assessment process; rating agencies often measure the same concept in different ways; ratings may paper over how the ratings system considers trade-offs among criteria, and ESG ratings do not consider shareholders' values.

The bulk of the SRI literature focuses on whether socially responsible investment decisions affect portfolio performance. The expectation is of a virtuous circle, where investors eschew unethical companies' stocks, thus reducing their access to capital and reducing their profitability. Oikonomou et al. (2019) find that institutional investors who are long-term in nature tend to have a positive relationship with CSR, thus companies are more likely to have stable investors if they act ethically. Yet, previous (mostly statistically-based) studies of returns show ambiguous results; simply put, *it's unclear whether it pays to be ethical*. For example, Badía et al. (2020) conclude, "SRI performance is geographically dependent, changes over time, and relies on the specific ESG screening strategy used […]." An OECD report finds no consistent evidence that ESG-compliant firms yield better returns, and some find that the returns are worse (Belghiatar et al. 2014; Brzeszczyński et al. 2019; Boffo and Patalano 2020). On the contrary, some studies such as that of

Trinks and Scholtens (2017) suggest that there is a clear cost to employing negative screening, implying that there is "profit in sin."

Climate change is the main catalyst behind the current push for ESG reporting harmonization. It has spurred the US Securities and Exchange Commission under the new (2021) Biden Administration to take notice of ESG standards,[3] as part of a push to regulate reporting in order to create more consistency. The new SEC team has looked into ESG investment disclosures and found them lacking. Their (SEC 2021, 4–5) report notes a number of serious issues around ESG investing. First, "portfolio management practices were inconsistent with disclosures about ESG approaches." They state that despite pronouncements about ethical investing, practice differed. In some cases, fund holdings are rife with low ESG score investments, and a general lack of follow-through in investment practices declaring ESG to guide decision-making. Second, "controls were inadequate to maintain, monitor, and update clients' ESG-related investing guidelines, mandates, and restrictions." The staff noted inadequate implementation of stated negative screens, such as investments in alcohol-selling companies, particularly when the directives behind the screens were ambiguous. Moreover, investor client preferences for certain types of industries were haphazardly followed, reflecting a lack of a monitoring system. Third, proxy voting was often inconsistent with advisors' state approaches. This relates to internal votes taken after ESG-related pronouncements were made (but often not followed). Fourth, there were "unsubstantiated or otherwise potentially misleading claims regarding ESG approaches." In some cases, the firms did not disclose payments received from ESG fund companies to promote their products. Fifth, there were inconsistencies between firms' ESG-related disclosures and marketing and firm practices. Here again, firms often did not follow through on their ESG promises. Sixth, there were inadequate compliance programs to address ESG issues. The report notes general challenges for companies to substantiate adherence to ESG processes, and thus raises general questions about the validity and reliability of ESG claims. Finally, the report notes a general lack of training and knowledge by compliance staff about ESG investment standards.

Very few academic articles have examined whether indices actually affect outcomes in terms of corporate behavior, but there are ample reasons to be

---

3 SEC Chair Gary Gensler publicly supported the need for a movement toward more consistent and regulated ESG reporting standards, particularly around climate change on July 28, 2021. See https://www.unpri.org/news-and-events/webinars-on-demand?commid=498753&utm_campaign=communication_reminder_24hr_registrants&utm_medium=email&utm_source=brighttalk-transact&utm_content=title, Accessed July 29, 2021.

skeptical, as we demonstrate in the next chapter. Chatterji et al. (2009) examine KLD environmental scores for companies against pollution emissions and penalties assessed in the United States and find that the index performs well in predicting the latter. However, they find it disturbing that KLD does not use historical performance indicators, which would have a greater predictive power. They also point to the problematic aspect of deciding which standard is "good" in terms of environmental performance. They emphasize that the indices and their study focus on "bad" behavior, ignoring positive steps companies might take to enhance performance. Perhaps more concerning is the lack of standardized data such as pollution outcomes in other countries.

Methodology of the SRI Indices: A Review

We now review the main SRI indices, to see how much transparency and accountability based on both the quality and methodology of the data are possible. We begin with a diagram that reflects the general methodological approach of the SRI ratings indices, based on our review of the methodologies of the systems noted further. Figure 3.1 reflects a great deal of ambiguity

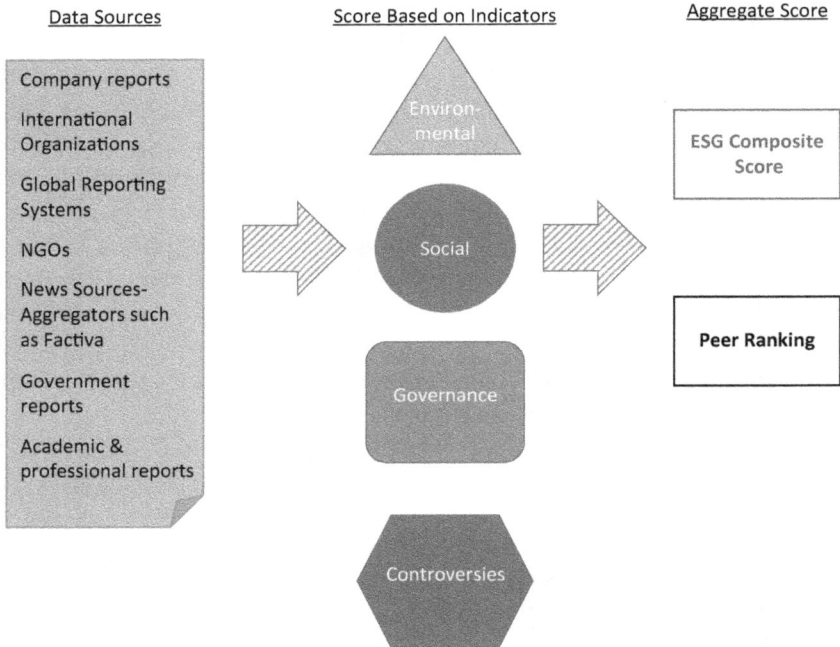

Figure 3.1 SRI Ratings Methodology—A Synthesis.
Source: Author.

in interpreting the validity and accuracy of reports because the ratings companies themselves depict their exact methodology, often including weighting of E versus S versus G, as proprietary knowledge. It is important to note that the exact indicators and peer review ranking are tailored by industry.

We now turn to a brief description of the leading ratings indices.

MSCI (KLD) ESG Ratings

KLD ratings offer ESG scores for large cap (capitalization, or relative value of stock) companies. KLD was the first widely used ESG ratings company, before being bought out by MSCI, an investment information and consulting service that offers financial performance and risk factor analysis to investor clients. MSCI bought out both KLD and Innovest ESG ratings services, combining them into the largest social ratings firm. Perrault and Quinn (2018) state that KLD is the most commonly used index by investors. According to their website (https://www.msci.com/our-solutions/esg-investing/esg-ratings, accessed June 16, 2021), the service had over 1,700 clients, "including leading pension funds, asset managers, consultants, advisers, banks, and insurers," and covers over 14,800 issuers and 680,000 equity and fixed income securities. Companies are rated as AAA, AA (leader); A, BBB, BB (average); and B, CCC (laggard). They explain to potential clients that ESG represents substantial risks to financial returns and are not easily monitored by normal indicators. They cite risks to water contamination, corruption, and/or safety risks for a mining company as an example. Scores are done on an industry basis. A sub-page of the website lays out the factors considered under each of the ESG pillars.[4] These include things like toxic waste under E; labor standards and community relations under S; and tax transparency under G. Curiously, corruption or host government relations are not included as separate factors under G. For each sector, these factors are given different weights to make up the overall score. For each company rated, they can provide a score for key weighted factors that can be translated into the laggard, average, and leader categories. All data are from publicly available sources; they give examples such as news articles; company disclosures; and GHG emissions and water quality reports.

What really stands out here is that they, like every other index, *do not gather primary data.* They do not visit or speak to local stakeholders on the ground. Nor do they examine company-government relations, or host government risk factors, such as corruption. Thus, they miss the entire political

---

4 https://www.msci.com/our-solutions/esg-investing/esg-ratings/esg-ratings-key-issue-framework, Accessed June 16, 2021.

landscape/context in which companies operate, outside of company-related events from news sources. These factors are at the heart of corporate controversies. Beyond these, this misses the opportunity to understand community perceptions toward large operations, such as mines, where hostility could create serious issues for company operations.

FTSE4Good Sustainability Index

The FTSE4Good index rates companies on the London Stock Exchange according to ESG criteria. It has parallel indices for emerging markets; an ASEAN index; an IBEX (Spain) index; and ones for Taiwan and Malaysia. There is an ESG Ratings as well as a Green Revenues index. We focus on the former here, as the latter seems oriented toward examining companies operating in the green economy. The website (https://www.ftserussell.com/data/sustainability-and-esg-data/esg-ratings, accessed June 16, 2021) states that it includes 7,200 securities in forty-seven different markets. It provides basic criteria for each of the ESG categories, including climate change and biodiversity under E; labor standards and human rights under S; and anti-corruption under governance. Community relations and host government behavior are again outside the scope of the index. The description of the index indicates that there are negative screens employed to not include companies producing certain products, such as tobacco and nuclear weapons.

As with KLD, the Guide to FTSE Sustainable Data states that all data are from publicly available sources.[5] Scores are given for performance in the criteria from 0 to 5, with 5 being best practice, and risk scores are given from 0 to 3, with 3 being high risk. There are over 300 indicators, which include both qualitative and quantitative indicators of management and corporate data disclosure, tailored for sector and geography. Non-company sources include NGOs such as the Ethical Trading Initiative, the International Labor Organization (ILO); International Organizations such as the International Finance Corporation; the World Bank; and the UN. There is no stakeholder engagement or assessment of country context or host government actions.

Mackenzie et al. (2013) find that threat of expulsion from the FTSE and engagement for remedial action have an effect on firm performance in regard to environmental management criteria. As with other studies, they also find that national and firm governance characteristics are important tempering

---

5 https://research.ftserussell.com/products/downloads/Guide_to_FTSE_Sustainable_Investment_Data_used_in_FTSE_Russell_Indexes.pdf, Accessed June 16, 2021.

variables. Charlo et al. (2015) find that belonging to the Spanish FTSE (IBEX) listing is associated with higher profits but more sensitivity to market shifts. On the other hand, Curran and Moran (2007) find that there is no positive effect for companies to be included in the FTSE4Good. Collison et al. (2009) echo those SRI critics in finding FTSE compliance is mostly performative. The managers they interviewed are concerned about the reputational effects of exclusion, at least for now, while most large firms are included, but are focused more with auditory compliance rather than changing behavior in any positive or transformative way.

Sustainalytics

Sustainalytics is another ESG index ratings company run by Morningstar, a large business information service. Their website (https://www.sustainalytics.com/, accessed June 16, 2021) suggests a similar approach as other services and covers over 4,500 companies across four industries. ESG risks are rated on a 40-point decile scale with 0–10 being negligible and 40+ being severe. There are twenty categories, including human rights, data privacy and security, corruption, community relations, and land use and biodiversity. As with the other indices, they examine companies within the context of each sector. The Methodology abstract (v. 2.1, January 2021), states that there are three basic building blocks that determine a company's rating: corporate governance, material ESG issues, and idiosyncratic ESG issues. Corporate governance includes measurement of the quality of management. Material issues include aspects such as employee safety. Idiosyncratic issues are "event-driven" and can be viewed as "black swan" events; examples given are the cancellation of the Keystone XL pipeline in the United States and the Pascua-Lama gold mine in Chile. The index appears to focus on how well companies manage sector-specific, event-driven, and geographic risk. While the specific data sources are not given, there is no systematic effort to conduct primary research such as interviewing stakeholders or examining host government factors beyond a general country risk.

Vigeo-Ethical Investor Research Service

Vigeo-Ethical Investor Research Service (EIRIS) offers investors ESG research and support, including assessment and ratings. The two services were merged in 2015; EIRIS stared in 1983, while Vigeo started in 2002. It is owned by business information service Moody's. Their website (https://vigeo-eiris.com/, accessed June 16, 2021) offers an assessment service for companies and sovereign country issues, designed to help reassure potential investors of the sustainability of their activities. They offer consulting advice to companies on how to improve ratings. They also offer three indices: the Euronext V.E. Index; the CAC 40 Governance Index; and the V.E. Best Emerging Market Performers Index (800 companies across thirty-one different countries). The Euronext V.E. index includes the 120 highest-ranking companies globally in terms of ESG performance. They offer a similar list broken down into EU country/regional markets and US-based companies.

The V.E. 2020 ESG Assessment Methodology reveals the following. There are thirty-eight ESG criteria based on forty unique data points. These appear to derive from the GRI, the Global Compact, the Paris Agreement on climate Change, ILO principles, and various other international agreements. These are given different weights based on the industry and are assessed according to three factors: leadership, implementation, and results. There are forty industry-specific "materiality assessments" that analyze the risk to stakeholders and companies of company activities. These are combined with company-specific management assessments around leadership, implementation, and results. This allows them to develop ESG scores that also highlight ESG controversies. The resulting overall ESG score spans from 0 (weak) to 100 (advanced) and is combined with a risk mitigation score to provide the overall ranking. Data sources include: corporate reporting; direct company contacts that are non-confidential, such as questionnaires; stakeholder websites; Factiva (owned by Dow Jones) press searches; and partnerships with stakeholder companies under review. V.E. appears to use Factiva, a database of news stories, to monitor company controversies. As with the other indices, V.E. uses only publicly available information.

Thomson Reuters Refinitiv

Thomson Reuters, a major publishing house and newswire, have a combined business news and analytics service which includes Refinitiv, an ESG index service. Refinitiv was reportedly sold to the London Stock Exchange Group in February 2021, however, it is still linked to the Thomson Reuters business news portal.[6] Like the other services, Refinitiv offers indices by sector as well as more specialized indices, such as the Future Super Australia fossil-free index, designed for pension funds and the Eurozone ESG Select Index. They also offer positive and negative screening for "criteria such as alcohol, armaments, carbon, and controversies in the media." They state that they

---

6 Shreya Tyagi, February 1, 2021, Thomson Reuters closes sale of Refinitiv to LSE, *SNL Financial Services Daily*, found at: Factiva news service, Accessed July 26, 2021.

use 450+ ESG metrics, with 186 comparable measures, that are customized by industry. The companies are rank ordered across ten category scores. As with the other indices, the exact methods and weighting are not transparent, however, they state that they use: annual reports; company websites; NGO websites; stock exchange filings; CSR reports; and new sources. They note that they have 150+ content research analysts across the globe (https://www.refinitiv.com/en/financial-data/indices/esg-index, and https://www.refinitiv.com/en/sustainable-finance/esg-investing, https://www.refinitiv.com/en/sustainable-finance/esg-scores, accessed July 26, 2021). Their methodology brief (2021) states that they cover 70% of the global market cap, with data dating from 2002. A lack of transparency on a key criterion by a company is negatively reflected in the ESG score. They also assign "severity weights" for controversial events. The ESG score comes from ESG factors, while the controversies score comes from controversies across ten different categories, aggregated into one score. Controversy data come from media reports as well as whether there have been any strikes during the period studied. These are then combined to create an ESG score (Refinitiv 2021).

Bloomberg

As noted above, perhaps the largest financial reporting business, Bloomberg, now offers its own ESG data. It relies on essentially the same data sources as the other indices, such as annual reports and third-party research, as well as the Bloomberg news feed. Scores on a 0–100 scale are marked by 800 different metrics that are tailored by sector. These are scored using a proprietary algorithm called the R-Factor™ that examines metrics that are "financially material" to potential returns (https://www.bloomberg.com/professional/product/indices/sasb/, https://www.bloomberg.com/professional/blog/opening-the-black-box-of-esg-data/, https://www.slideshare.net/FrameworkLLC/what-is-a-bloomberg-esg-score, accessed July 26, 2021).

Limitations of Ratings Methodologies

We have reviewed the general approach and methodologies of the leading SRI indices and found similarities. The ratings seem to be comprehensive in coverage, including all large companies listed in any major stock exchange. All identify certain criteria and indicators for assessment, employing an accounting approach to checkbox company reporting and to examine "adverse" events through news databases, which are then written up as an episode diary (generally about one paragraph) in the "controversies" score. In regard to more objective and widely reported upon indicators, such as those required by domestic Western authorities, the ratings data are a good compendium of corporate behavior in certain areas of interest, such as emissions. However, controversies are monitored mainly by the number of (largely Western) news reports around a certain incident, and sometimes given a general category for level of seriousness, rather than an examination of the longevity, complexity, tractability, or company response to the episode.

By keeping controversies separate from a lot of self-reported indicators, they mix up subjective and objective information of varying quality. For example, many of the indicators are "true/false" or "pass/fail" such as whether a company has a human rights policy. Nor is there any reflection on the differences in reporting across countries, such as the poor level of disclosures by, or reporting on, Chinese state-dominated firms. Some reporting agencies claim to run audits, and to consult with management, but the extent of such efforts is impossible to discern. Multiple reports are taken as validity of the importance of the event, not the quality of information. No attempt is made to look on the ground at serious ongoing events to understand their nature and seriousness. More fundamentally, it is not clear how they choose which criteria to include, but the many indicators reflect a huge reporting burden for companies.

Each company is generally given an overall grade that follows academic standards, A being outstanding, B competent, C weak, and D failing. Some ratings use multiple letters, such as AAA (highest) versus AA (second highest) versus A (third highest) to match bond ratings. The sources of the overall company score and of how much a particular indicator affects an E, S, or G score are opaque, so the system is essentially a "pass/fail" one in which companies just have to avoid major scandals to be viewed as ethical actors. Similarly, where sample weights are given, the reasons for weighting one indicator or overall factor over another are not explained.

In fact, much of the discussion in the methodological brochures focuses on "risk exposure," indicating that the primary purpose for the reporting is to avoid risks. This reflects a private and investment sector *seeking to avoid scandals, not recognize ethical behavior.* Notice that *there are no primary data, stakeholder engagement, or examination of facts on the ground. None are transparent in their weighting,* though that may change. *Essentially, they are designed to give a ready number and/or letter score that allows a money manager to principally focus on return on investment,* which is clearly the driving evaluation criterion if we judge by how pension fund managers depict their performance. In fact, every indicator methodology we have seen emphasizes the *centrality of financial materiality* as the reason for inclusion.

There is *no way for them to engage in "positive" screening in such a way as to monitor and incentivize changes in corporate or sectoral behavior over the long-run.* This brings up the question, what about the large pension funds? They should be able to shape and mold the SRI indices' design, to make it responsive to their needs. To reflect upon that question, we turn to a mini case study of CalPERS, perhaps the most activist pension fund in the world, and how it states it uses ratings to guide its investment decisions.

CalPERS: An Example of an Activist Pension Fund's Perspective

If there are some reporting gaps in the SRI ratings agencies, as we reviewed above, surely the largest pension funds can create supplemental information to inform their weighty decisions about which companies they want to invest in. Perhaps the largest pension fund holder in the world is the California Public Employees' Retirement System (CalPERS), a member of PRI. According to its Investment & Pension Funding Facts at a Glance for FY 2019–20, its fund was valued at $392.5 billion in 2020, with a return of 4.7% that year. According to the Facts for FY 2019–20 "About CalPERS," it had operating costs of $626.5 million, including 2,843 personnel, and another $994.7 million in investment costs (management and administration) going to external agents in FY 2020–21. CalPERS' website includes a sub-page from their Sustainable Investments team (https://www.calpers.ca.gov/page/investments/sustainable-investments-program/esg-integration, accessed June 16, 2021). The page states four key goals:

- Assess and manage high-value ESG risks and opportunities alongside traditional factors in the investment process.
- Review, pilot, procure, and/or create useful tools to facilitate integration of high-value ESG topics into investment processes.
- Recognize profitable opportunities based on ESG characteristics and those considered most at risk from shifts toward more sustainable products and services.
- Identify ways to generate positive social and environmental impact with strong financial returns. We call these "Why Wouldn't You?" opportunities.

What stands out here is the idea of using investment to effect positive change as opposed to just avoiding risk, however, how positive change is enabled is not explained. The page instead offers a link to an online Sustainable Investment Research Initiative Library. This contains links to papers, mostly from academic journals on ESG questions, with little information on CalPERS' decisions or own investigations. Most of the articles require payment or library subscription to access.

Limited information about their investment practices can be gleaned from downloadable pdf documents from this main webpage. The Global Equity: Sustainable Investment Practice Guidelines document (no date) notes that the Aggregate Portfolio includes over 10,000 securities in forty-seven markets with a market value of $160 billion, which includes 50% of all assets. It suggests that portfolio managers must monitor ESG issues, but does not specify how. The baseline source of information is the MSCI ESG rating. The 2019 CalPERS' Governance & Sustainability Principles include diversity in corporate boards and the need for regulatory effectiveness. Regulatory effectiveness includes factors around the financial system, as well as political stability, including civil liberties, political risks such as conflict and corruption; and freedom of the press; and labor rights.

CalPERS created a Focus List of the approximately ten worst corporate performers in terms of both financial performance and corporate governance in 1992, but *decided to end this "naming and shaming" approach in 2010, despite arguments from its management team that it had led to corporate performance improvements*, including through CalPERS providing guidance to companies (Anson et al. 2003).

It has instead created its own SRI index, the Permissible Country Index as a screening mechanism. CalPERS began considering non-financial risks in 1999 when it asked Wilshire Consulting to revise its screening index to consider political risk as well as market factors, including volatility, investor protection, capital market openness, and transaction costs (Soederberg 2007). These were expanded in the early 2000s to begin considering other factors in response to growing activism. Political stability includes democracy, including civil rights and the independence of the judiciary. According to Soederberg, Wilshire's determination of the quality of democracy draws from the Contracts and Law Sub-index of the Global Competitiveness Report of the World Economic Forum, and the International Country Risk Guide of the PRS consultancy in the United States. The latter scores political risk from a 1–3 scale, with 3 being "good." Countries with less than 2 are taken out of the eligible list. Other factors include transparency in the press and in financial reporting, and "productive labor practices," which refers to ILO standards. Assessment of labor is based upon reporting by Verité, a US-based non-profit reporting organization. Such assessments led to CalPERS pulling investment from the Philippines, Thailand, Indonesia, and Malaysia, in response to labor and human rights standards. It appears to have discontinued country screening in 2008 in favor of a principles-based approach as described above (Eccles and Sesia 2009). In short, CalPERS has pulled back from the main lever it had to create a serious screen for its concerned pension fund holders, and one that could have offered real consequences for countries engaged in serial human rights abuses.

Conclusion

It is understandable why SRI indices are attractive to investment managers. They are supposed to translate comprehensive information into a ready-to-use quantified ranking that money managers can plug into their investment calculations. Yet, we have seen that their methods are inherently limited to publicly available, secondary information that may be biased and effectively reflect a selective echo chamber. Even smaller ratings firms with strong reputations and ties to NGOs, such as Covalence, which presents the Peacebuilding Index listing the 300 most positive impact companies, rely on web-based information.[7] As *The Economist* noted in 2018, while ESG reporting services are gaining traction, the standards and methods around them are a "hodgepodge."[8] In fact, there is scant academic literature on the indices, and almost no comprehensive tests of their validity, accuracy, accurate representation, or consistency, no doubt hampered by the lack of transparency in (proprietary) methodology and data sources and usage as well as their relative novelty. Simply put, institutional investors have to trust the rating agencies' assessments.

Moreover, there is no assurance that the ratings companies, most of which are linked to large financial services companies, won't suffer from the same conflict of interest as the credit ratings agencies who performed miserably thus contributing to the 2008 global financial crash (Hira et. al, 2013). Similar to the 2008 crash, companies can certainly influence the scoring of their performance by rigging their company reports and influencing media coverage. As discussed in regard to examining the reality of mining CSR through on the ground investigation (Hira and Busumtwi-Sam 2021), reporting may be quite alien to the reality facing communities on the ground who are dealing with large multinationals. In one instance, in Western Ghana, I found a mining company that had won numerous international awards for its CSR was almost universally despised within the community, including being seen as damaging to the environment and not interested in democratic governance or community development as reflected in dozens

---

7 https://www.covalence.ch/, Accessed June 21, 2021.
8 Green tape, *The Economist*, 426,9084 (2018): 76.

of stakeholder interviews and a wide survey of local citizens by a local firm employed by the researchers. This is typical of my experience with visiting a number of mining companies across the South that are highly rated by global reporters but despised by local citizens. It explains why there continue to be hundreds of mining conflicts around the world, a number that shows no sign of diminishing even after decades of purported CSR investments and the construction of all the CSR reporting regimes and ESG reporting industry.[9] Surely this suggests some public regulation of such information would be necessary to ensure its quality and truthful fiduciary responsibility of companies, reporting agencies, and investment managers. Without reforming the reporting system, CSR and ESG will remain a smoke and mirrors kabuki performance for an audience that is familiar with its inherent flaws, according to a number of pension fund and ESG managers with whom I shared the analysis of this book.

We have furthermore seen that while data sources for ratings sometimes include Western media reporting, it makes no effort to talk to local populations in the South who are directly affected by and can affect company operations, or to host governments who are equal partners. There is misplaced faith in the idea that all marginalized people across the world have access to Western media and that their stories are accurately and thoroughly reported. Even in democratic societies, there is often a fear of repression and retribution amidst social and political tensions, which I have seen firsthand in terms of efforts to censor my own studies of mining CSR. In short, such indices make no effort to understand the context of corporate activity and views of the stakeholders, which is not well-captured by one-off news stories. Such stories are a freeze frame of what's happening at any given point, rather than an examination of an unfolding story of corporate and host government negotiations, development of an agreement with local and global stakeholders, issues arising, and how communities, governments, and companies respond to those issues. Of the ratings services we examined, only MSCI (KLD) claimed to track singular events over time. We found some evidence of this when we obtained the current (2021) MSCI report for Barrick Gold. The report appropriately flagged ongoing issues in Pascua Lama, Tanzania, and Papua New Guinea, yet there have not been any ramifications for the company's stock price.

Ratings methods are treated as proprietary information, thus it would be hard to verify the accuracy, consistency, reliability, and validity of such constructs that inevitably require some value judgments in weighting different factors. It is impossible to say

---

9 See https://www.ocmal.org/, for a current list of mining conflicts in Latin America.

what money managers would focus on, in other words, even if there are reports of violations in one part of the entire ESG report. Perrault and Quinn (2018) state that singular indicators via a composite index (overall rank) tend to obscure many important and potentially significant aspects of stakeholder relations. They note, "the single CSP (corporate social performance) score smothers perceptions that stakeholders may hold regarding the firm's positive and negative performance on a dimension of CSP, muddying its connection to FP (financial policy)." Thus, even if KLD was able to capture a serious adverse event over time through global news aggregators, without primary investigation, it would not reflect the true context and views of local workers and communities on the ground, nor would it capture the effectiveness of a company's response to such problems, rendering such efforts fruitless in terms of offering sound information to investors. Thus, the company would not suffer any ramifications of its ethical violations, which is what the CSR/ESG system is designed for. As we have seen with the case of CalPERS, there is no indication of any serious push or independent investigation by the pension funds themselves to improve the quality of the information by the reporting agencies. All parties, the companies, the reporting agencies, and the investment managers, rather seem cozy with focusing on avoiding major scandals, or waiting for them to pass, rather than improving corporate behavior. To make sure we are not missing anything, we took a deep dive into actual serious and ongoing adverse events and issues, to see how they played out through the rating system. We turn in the next chapter to our findings.

Chapter 4

HOW HUMAN RIGHTS VIOLATIONS ARE SYSTEMATICALLY DOWNPLAYED IN SRI SYSTEMS

Serious Human Rights Issues Should Be Reflected in ESG Ratings

Understanding that the socially responsible investment (SRI) methodologies are designed to offer assessments of the ethical performance of a company, as a logical next step, we would want to see if "adverse" corporate events involving conflicts by corporations are adequately reflected in both the news sources upon which SRI indices rely and in their ratings of companies. There are very few studies of the environment, social, and governance (ESG) impact, as opposed to correlations with financial returns. Li and Wu (2020) use data from RepRisk, a Swiss-based company that offers ESG data. Its website states that "machine learning algorithms" are used to identify ESG risks, vetted through a team of 100+ analysts (https://www.reprisk.com/, accessed July 28, 2021). Its subpage describing its process indicates that it does not gather primary data. The authors find that after firms joined the Global Compact, the number of negative events they were involved in declined by 50%. This largely holds for private but not for publicly owned companies. Overall, however, they find that *Global Compact signatory companies did not have different ESG profiles from nonparticipants*, suggesting factors other than the Compact are driving performance. They further find that downstream companies closer to consumers have fewer ESG incidents. Private firms that were expelled from the Compact had an increase in negative ESG incidents, but there was no change for public companies. The authors note that positive ESG incidents are far less likely to be captured by the events data than negative ones. They also note that ESG responsiveness declines where there are conflicts with societies and shareholders, thus implying that ESG indicators are reflecting existing behavior rather than shifting it. Overall, they conclude that *there is no case to be made that corporate social responsibility (CSR)/ESG leads to improved outcomes*.

In order to provide a further test to the extensive findings discussed thus far, we examine the three problematic sectors of mining, electronics, and apparel/footwear, which are the most common industry subjects of media attention in regard to CSR. We chose these sectors because they are "downstream" output industries that are close to consumers, as opposed to upstream input industries such as chemicals or steel, and so much more likely to elicit attention by pension fund managers. Moreover, all three sectors have been mired in occasional scandals over the past few decades, from widespread media reporting about suicides by Apple workers to the sweatshop allegations around the apparel and footwear industry. The mining industry has perhaps no parallel in terms of the number of ongoing conflicts at the community level, including a growing number of lawsuits alleging human rights violations occurring in the South being taken up in Western courts. Simply put, if these three most highlighted sectors are not following SRI principles, it's hard to believe any of the other more underreported sectors are either. To provide flesh-and-bones examples of issues in the sectors, we begin with three mini cases of recent corporate scandals that attracted global attention.

Mini Case Studies of Ongoing CSR Issues

While media sources are geared toward immediate scandals, an on-the-ground observer sees patterns of problems across time and space. The failure of companies to address nagging issues is illustrated in a series of mini cases, derived from our review of neutral sources above. The cases demonstrate that *what might appear in media stories to be one-off issues are more like symptoms of nagging problems*, ones that the current CSR reporting system is not equipped to deal with.

Pascua Lama

Pascua Lama was a proposed open pit mining project proposed by Barrick gold on the border of Chile and Argentina in the southern part of the Atacama Desert that would have yielded rich deposits of gold, silver, and copper. The timing of the project proposal derives from the 1997 signing of The Mining Integration and Complementation Treaty between Chile and Argentina that permitted projects straddling the border to enjoy relaxation from national laws. The project has been mired in controversy since its proposal in 2000, due to environmental concerns related to glaciers around the site area. The valley is a rich agricultural area, and both local and global NGOs and protestors claimed that Barrick had not completed a thorough environmental impact study, with particular concern for effects on water. Several rounds of environmental studies and assessments by both

Barrick and the Chilean National Environmental Commission (CONAMA), alongside lawsuits seeking to halt the project took place over the 2000s. These include a new environmental impact study presented by Barrick in 2004 for an enlarged plan. Local residents, including indigenous groups, felt alienated from the formal regulatory process and the challenges of responding to a technical document; CONAMA was only required to hear their complaints for a 60-day period. Approval was gained in Chile and Argentina by 2006. The project budget as of 2009 was estimated at $3 billion, when construction started (Urkidi 2010; Urkidi and Walter 2011).

Construction was suspended in 2013 due to rising protests and costs, which were estimated at $8.5 billion by then. In 2014, Barrick was fined $16 million over noncompliance with regulatory requirements. Barrick accepted the decision of the (Chilean) Antofagasta Environmental Court to close the mine in 2020 (Engineering & Mining Journal 2020). As Haslam (2018) explains, institutional, legal, and regulatory differences explain why action to stop the mine was effective in Chile but not in Argentina, however, for all intents and purposes the project is dead. Nonetheless, in 2019, Argentina's Supreme Court upheld its glacier protection law, which creates additional barriers to mining in the region. Especially important for the outcome was the championing by the Latin American Observatory of Environmental Conflicts (OLCA) in the Chilean capital. OLCA was able to recast the Chilean environmental impact reporting by Barrick and take advantage of evolving Chilean environmental institutions in response to growing public concerns (Cortez and Maillet 2018; Haslam and Godfrid 2020). As Maher et al. (2019) point out, the decision by such governments should be seen as a complex discourse through which the interplay of state, company, and community unfolds. While Barrick attempted to offer payoffs to the community, including local expenditures on public services and other forms of co-optation, and reached out both to local indigenous protestors and farmers to change their opinions, their principal action was focused on convincing the state of the payoffs of the project, and then pursuing legal recourse when protestors put pressure on the state to halt the project. The increase in protests over time explains the fluidity and seeming contradictions of state reactions to the project. In the end, Barrick had to write off half a billion dollars in lost investment.[1] There is nothing in ESG indices to indicate investors had any warning about this dramatic loss.

---

1 Paul Christopher Weber, 2019. A Long Road: For decades, Canadian mining operations have wreaked havoc in developing countries. Villages have been razed, water supplies poisoned and allegations of rape—even murder—have emerged. But finally, there is hope for a way out. Could a new avenue for justice lead to a brighter future for all of our mines? *Report on Business Magazine.* February: p. 20.

This incident was not isolated; Barrick has had serious issues around mines in Tanzania and Papua New Guinea as well. These suggest high risk propensity, and inadequate systems to gain community trust and develop local partners. What comes across is a calculation around local resistance to mining, with CSR/ESG being a very secondary factor, to be overcome at minimal cost in the process of developing the project. Clearly, CSR competencies need to go well beyond reporting activities to navigate such challenging conditions, however, there is nothing forcing companies to develop such competencies. As a result, the same issues are faced over and over again in the mining industry with no evidence of a learning curve. As noted with Barrick's loss, incompetence in community relations is financially material.

Vale Mariana Tailings Dam Disaster

Vale, the privatized Brazilian mining giant, was responsible for one of the worst mining disasters when its tailings (residues, often toxic) dam failed near Mariana, Minas Gerais, in Brazil on November 5, 2015. The spill killed nineteen people, swamping two nearby towns, a major river, and the Atlantic Ocean outlets with toxic sludge. As noted above, the Samarco mine was a joint venture between Vale and Australian giant BHP Billiton, with each company owning 50%. In January 2019, another Vale tailings dam, near Brumadinho, Brazil, also failed, killing 259 people, with another eleven missing. The company agreed to pay $7 billion in compensation for the Brumadinho disaster. Criminal charges were also filed against Vale and German safety inspector Tüv Süd.[2] According to the *Wall Street Journal*, Tüv Süd had clear conflicts of interest, as it had received additional contracts for consulting from, and co-authored research reports with, Vale.[3] Vale needs to spend an estimated $1.3 billion to retrofit similar dams in order to prevent similar disasters from potentially happening (Jensen 2019). The whole event reveals once again the dangerous conflicts of interest rife in CSR reporting. A company can be reporting positive earnings and ESG indicators for years while neglecting fundamental safety protocols, which eventually leads to catastrophic failure. There is nothing in the CSR reporting system, based on media, NGO, and company reporting, that deals with such long-term slowly evolving issues.

---

2 BBC, Vale dam disaster: $7billion compensation for disaster victims, February 4, 2021, found at: https://www.bbc.com/news/business-55924743, Accessed August 13, 2021.
3 Jeffrey Lewis and Paulo Trevisani, Vale Dam Auditor Told Police He Felt Pressured to Attest to Safety of Dam: The Auditor Said the Company Knew of the Risks Days before the Collapse, *The Wall Street Journal*, February 7, 2019.

The incident highlights another core problem with CSR reporting efforts, that is, they fail to consider the regulatory capacity of host governments, as reflected in the inability to respond adequately with regulatory remediation to the first dam burst (Hira 2020b). The fact that host governments are not reporting on their use of revenues or their community relations is a huge gap that can lead to major dissonance against companies, particularly when the community feels it is not being adequately protected by national regulators and/or receiving adequate benefits from companies. It is baffling that companies are willing to spend millions on CSR efforts and reporting to gain community acceptance, yet they completely ignore the capacity of local governments who deliver the public services that will improve people's lives. In the absence of capable government, the company effectively self-regulates, raising suspicions by observers, local and global, and is forced to take on the role of delivering public services such as education and health care, that are beyond their capacity and for which they are unaccountable creating a "governance paradox" (Hira and Busumtwi-Sam 2021).

Apple/Foxconn Suicides

Foxconn (whose parent company is Taiwan-based Hon Hai Precision Industry Company), is the lead manufacturer for a number of IT and electronics firms, including Apple, Microsoft, HP, Samsung, and Sony, experienced a rash (14) of suicides from 2010 at its Chinese factories. The suicides revealed Apple and other Western firms' deep dependence on Foxconn, a relationship that continues, despite Apple shifting some limited contracts to another subcontracting firm, Pegatron. Foxconn is a challenge as well for the Chinese state. It is the largest industrial employer, reportedly with more than one million employees from 2010. The conditions at Foxconn factories are lamentably unfamiliar to most Western consumers who lap up their products. They are self-contained with dormitories and security guards. The guards obstruct the movement of workers in and out of the compound, as Apple and Foxconn are concerned about losing trade secrets. Workers work minimal twelve-hour days, and the dorms reportedly offer substandard living conditions, such as frequent electricity and water shortages. Dorms are needed as most of the workers are from rural areas and are bound to the company under China's migration system. Workers are isolated from those not working in their sections. There are reports of strong disciplinary actions on workers, including violent beatings.

As in the fashion industry, tight control reflects tight shipping deadlines for large volumes of product with airtight quality expectations. Apple's profit margins are far higher than Foxconn's and it can squeeze its partners with timelines and reducing budgets. Apple's response to the suicides was to demand remedial action from Foxconn, sending an auditing team in 2011 to verify changes, including offering counseling and large suicide nets to deter workers from jumping off the roof. In 2012, Apple joined the Fair Labor Association (FLA), which provided a third-party audit. It's important to note as an aside that FLA audits were not included in the present study because its board is dominated by corporations. Foxconn also raised wages at its factories. Nonetheless when increasing pressure from Apple in 2012 for defect-free iPhones in short-turnaround time led to workers working around the clock every day, over 3,000 workers went on strike on October 5, in the Foxconn Zhengzhou plant. The Chinese government, in turn, promised direct elections for union representatives in 2013, and to uphold Chinese trade union law (Chan et al. 2013; Pun et al. 2016).

The important point here is that even if the suicides have ceased, the underlying conditions of worker exploitation and intense control have not changed. Raising wages does little to alleviate the spartan living conditions or overwork tension created by Foxconn's approach, and ultimately, Apple's supply chain demands. This is not surprising given that the CSR system is premised on monitoring one-off news stories. While the *New York Times* covered this story widely, for example, it did not have the scope or depth to probe deeper causes around global electronics supply chain issues in its coverage (Guo et al. 2012). Similar exploitative working conditions abound around the industrial belt in South China, which more recent wage increases and haphazard labor rights enforcement do little to address (Lüthje and Butollo 2017). Clarke and Boersma (2017) point to a series of independent investigations of Apple's supply chain that clearly demonstrate environmental and labor issues persist, in spite of the company's claims to have addressed them. As of November 2022, new worker protests broke out at Apple factories in China, underscoring that, despite years of ESG reporting, the company has failed to solve the underlying problems. Such issues should be of great interest to investors who are genuinely concerned about ESG as opposed to avoiding scandals, but apparently, the ESG reporting system enables investors to ignore persistent issues, even after exposure by one of the world's leading news sources.

Rana Plaza Factory Collapse

On April 24, 2013, the Rana Plaza building collapsed, including a clothing factory, killing an estimated 1,134 and injuring 2,600. The factory was one of a series of similar events in Bangladesh, where an estimated 4.4 million people work to make apparel at an estimated $0.32 an hour, collectively accounting for some 80% of national exports. Labor repression prevents the ability to form strong unions.[4] With the help in some cases of clothing brand labels found in the rubble, two different temporary (five-year) agreements were signed by the Western clothing companies involved with the factory to improve conditions. The Alliance for Bangladesh Worker Safety includes members such as Walmart, the Gap, Target, Hudson's Bay, Saks Fifth Avenue, and Lord & Taylor. The Accord on Fire and Building Safety, including American Eagle, H&M, and Inditex (Zara) offers a stronger legal statement about responsibility to create safe work environments. Both offered a series of audits of subcontractor factories and training to ensure worker safety. In addition, a $30 million compensation fund was set up for victims.

However, as Hira (2017) points out, the auditing systems do not catch all possible subcontractors; the reports are limited and incomplete; and there is no real enforcement mechanism on either the companies or the factory owners to ensure remediation of safety issues found. There is, furthermore, disharmony in terms of factory and audit coverage between the two agreements. Neither provides funding for remediation, thus local factory owners are more likely to choose evasion than costly upgrading. Clear unevenness and conflicts of interest with the consulting firms contracted out to audit the factories abound, as the firms live on further contracts from the companies. The system as a whole does not focus on the weakest link, namely the lack of government capacity or will to enforce basic safety or labor standards, similar to the mining industry.

More recently, the Accord, having completed its five-year mandate, transitioned to a private RMG Sustainability Council (RSC). The RSC is to take on the functions of inspections and training. However, the council is dominated by the Bangladesh Garment Manufacturers and Export Association, which represents factory owners, though it formally works with foreign companies and the government's factory inspection unit (Directory of Inspection of Factory and Establishment). It does not have anything close to the $11 million per year budget of the Accord. The successor to the Alliance, Nirapon, provides inspections and advice but has no ability to require remediation for problems found (Trebilcock 2020).

While recent assessments point to improvements in factory safety as a result of the Accord and Alliance efforts, their non-renewal brings such progress into peril. The experiments show that putting resources and effort into safety do have payoffs, however, they also reveal that the power

---

4 Dana Thomas, Why Won't We Learn from the Survivors of the Rana Plaza Disaster? *The New York Times*, found at: https://www.nytimes.com/2018/04/24/style/survivors-of-rana-plaza-disaster.html, Accessed August 16, 2021.

asymmetries among factory owners, the government, and multinationals within the context of continuing fast fashion protocols (low prices and short deadlines) means that only multinationals can really provide the resources and impetus for change (Rahman and Rahman 2020). Thus far, they have shown no sustained interest in offering longer-term contracts with fixed factories that would likely raise their prices or change the fundamental nature of precarious and shifting supply chains. *Nor is there any real change in the status of workers*, who remain unable to effectively collectively organize. In fact, just an estimated 3% of garment workers are unionized, and there remain a series of regulatory and political barriers to that changing (Bair et al. 2020).

None of this complexity will show up in an SRI ESG index. More to the point, Jacobs and Singhai (2017) could find *no* stock market reaction in terms of share prices for Western companies' involvement with the disaster (prices for their sample of thirty-nine affected firms went down on the day of the disaster, but then rebounded) *or* to the announcement of the Accord and Alliance. Contrary to Rahman and Rahman (2020), they find the profitability of local factory owners to be on par with their large multinational partners, thus the failure is in local government enforcement, not a lack of resources. The authors conclude "the stock market reaction suggests that investors do not hold retailers responsible for the Rana Plaza disaster and also do not see much, if any, reputational damage from the incident."

Islam et al. (2018) conducted a study of external auditors involved in the apparel business in Bangladesh shortly after the Rana Plaza disaster that sheds important general light on why auditors miss basic facts on the ground for workers. They note, for example, that most external auditors are hired by companies in reaction to a perceived legitimacy crisis (often linked to a report by a Western NGO) and/or as a requirement from a buyer, and are seen as an effective way of defusing it. They tend to closely follow company audit guidelines, such as completing all interview work within a day, and not speaking to external parties or communicating audit results with workers. More importantly, there is no effort by auditors to see if previous efforts have led to any real changes on the ground. The authors conclude (31): "Thus, a social compliance audit becomes a ritualistic practice that supports MNCs' maintenance of legitimacy to the wider community rather than creating real accountability [...]," continuing

> At a minimum, the social compliance audits comprise two quite different characters. For most of its life, it is a calming, routinized, maintenance of both order and the appearance of order. The audit is a successful combination of a problem-simplifying technology, of routine and superficiality but bound around with a language and aura of symbolic

legitimacy and an appeal through its panopticon character to the threat of real economic penalty. This ritual is played out and is both legitimated by and helps legitimate the surrogates' suggested codes (such as ILO's ones) and guidelines that successfully convey a notion of appropriate beneficence that the MNCs are happy to exploit through their reporting and other information dissemination mechanisms. There is an entirely other audit process when surrogates' sanction (such as NGOs' protest resulting in labor unrest or media's highlight of child labor) is mobilised—when the maintenance of "*normal*" has failed. The symbolic legitimacy of the "external auditor" is then called upon and their "professional" symbolic legitimacy is brought to bear in the fire-fighting, deflecting surrogates' sanction and criticism and repairing legitimacy. And these more serious and more substantial auditors engage a wider range of surrogates (including NGOs, media, local community, labor leaders)—although whether to be seen to do so; whether in order to identify and defuse trouble-makers; or whether for both purposes was unclear to us. There is nothing in the audit process which is actually designed to accept surrogates' voices and identify and reduce the risk of the MNCs. There is simply not enough work undertaken for the real risks—whether to workers or to the MNCs to emerge and/or to be identified.

Methodology: Tracing How Serious Human Rights Scandals (Deaths) Are Reported in and Affect Ratings

We wanted to do more than just review corporate scandals. We want to know whether the CSR ESG ratings systems are accurately reporting serious allegations of corporate abuse, and how such reports are affecting the ratings. Simply put, we should expect that serious disasters such as the previous mini cases should lead to major negative ratings. This would confirm that the ratings system is working well.

To find serious negative corporate events, we rely on data from third-party (neutral) sources that monitor corporate behavior with no apparent conflict of interest in regard to contracts with companies to report on their behavior. If we simply examined the same news sources that ESG reporters rely upon, such as Factiva, we would end up simply reproducing the same results, though they might not be adequately reflected in the ratings. The real question is whether these secondary news sources upon which ratings firms rely are accurate and thorough to reflect the reality of corporate social relations, as well as being reflected in a meaningful way upon ESG ratings. We first examined the two readily available datasets through our university library subscriptions: Factiva and Thomson Reuters. Factiva is a commonly cited source by SRI indices as a source for news stories about companies and Thomson Reuters is a leading business data source that offers its own ESG ratings of companies.

We then focus our attention on the more problematic challenge of reporting on conditions in the global South, where media is less likely to be developed and to enjoy the same civil liberties and resources as their counterparts in the North, to see if Factiva and Thompson Reuters are capturing all serious incidents. Unlike data on state-led repression or violence, around which there are multiple datasets, there are (curiously) no reliable datasets on global corporate behavior. The ILO reports on incidents, such as strikes, but does not link them to specific corporations, as its purpose is to monitor labor laws. The closest thing to a database is the Business & Human Rights Resource (BHRR) (https://www.business-humanrights.org/en/, accessed July 22, 2021), which compiles press and NGO stories of allegations about company abuses. However, their search function has limitations in that it only offers links to stories, rather than datapoints, and its Boolean functionality is limited. We have sorted the stories by sector, searching for the key terms "killings" or "deaths." We selected only these most egregious human rights violations for the simple reason that expanding the search would have yielded far too many results. Our purpose here is only to test whether the ESG information system works to provide accurate information to pension fund managers, so tracing how a selection of the most egregious incidents works its way through the system is sufficient. We conducted the search for the period from January 1, 2010 to January 1, 2019.

Given the limitations of that BHRR database, we supplemented it by creatively finding other sector-specific data reporters that allow for searches by abuse-sector time period, rather than the general one-off stories that abound on NGO websites. We select only sources that appear to have solid institutional backing in terms of financing and whose main purpose is to provide information based on primary, on-the-ground sources on CSR. By using multiple sources with primary data on the ground, we are able to triangulate stories that have solid grounding and therefore should be reflected in SRI indices and investment decisions. *Please see Appendix A for the full database of companies linked to major human rights, labor, and/or environmental violations.* Each sector summary lists the companies who appear on multiple lists.

Mining

For the mining sector, we searched BHRR for the words "killings" and "deaths" for multiple stories or reports from January 1, 2010 to January 1, 2019 (accessed July 22, 2021). There were 673 citations, so we only perused the headlines for companies accused of human rights, labor, or environmental violations. In our summary in Table 4.1, we include all companies with multiple entries over multiple years. See Appendix A for the full list. We also examined conflicts reported by the Environmental Justice Atlas (EJAtlas) (https://ejatlas.org/, accessed July 20, 2021). The EJAtlas reports on global conflicts around resource extraction and is backed by the European Union (EU).

Table 4.1 List of Major Mining Companies: Alleged Violent Incidents by Multiple Primary Reporting Sources

Company	HQ Country	Countries of Alleged Violations & Years
Rio Tinto	Australia	Mozambique, Papua New Guinea (2013–14, 2017)
OceanaGold	Australia	Philippines (2016); El Salvador (2018)
Vale/BHP	Brazil/Australia	Brazil (2015–present), major tailings dam failure
Barrick	Canada	Chile (2001); Peru (2002); Tanzania, Papua New Guinea (2010–18)
Goldcorp	Canada	Guatemala (2005–17)
Fortuna Silver Minerals	Canada	Mexico (2012–18)
Tahoe Resources	Canada	Guatemala (2010–17), Escobal mine
HudBay Minerals	Canada	Guatemala (2010–17)
Anvil Mining	Canada (Chinese own %)	DRCongo (2010–15)
Harmony Gold	South Africa	South Africa (2012–18)
Lonmin	South Africa	South Africa (2012–18)
Anglo American	South Africa	South Africa (2013–18), silicosis/TB case
AngloGold Ashanti	South Africa	South Africa (2013–18), silicosis/TB case
Gold Fields	South Africa	South Africa (2013–18), silicosis/TB case
Glencore Xstrata	Switzerland	Peru (2015), Philippines (2014), DRC (2012–14)
Vedanta	UK	India (2018–19)
Newmont	US	Peru (2004–13)
Drummond Mining	US	Colombia (2011–16)

Sources: Appendix A.

There is a total dataset of 3,490 global conflicts reported. We used the following filters to reduce the cases to the most egregious and conflictual ones around corporate behavior: mineral ores and building materials extraction (sector filter); high intensity (widespread, mass mobilization, violence, arrests, etc. [...]); deaths, assassinations, murders, violent targeting of activists; and repression. This yielded twenty-six cases reported on the Atlas. The conflicts from EJAtlas highlighted in Appendix A were verified again on OCMAL, the Latin American Observatory for Mining Conflicts (https://www.ocmal. org/, accessed July 20, 2021).

Apparel

Tracking labor and human rights violations in the textile, clothing, and footwear industries is extremely problematic given the byzantine and ever-shifting system of subcontracts from the major brands to clothing factories (Hira 2017). We examined the BHRR database, searching for "deaths" or "killings" for the clothing and textile and footwear industries for 2010–19. Human Rights Watch (www.hrw.org, accessed July 21, 2021) also produces reports on a periodic basis. The reports tend to be thematic and thus do not lend themselves easily to search for specific rights allegations abuses by companies. However, a HRW (2015) report published by them on the Cambodian garment industry revealed widespread labor abuses. They found such abuse to be widespread across the industry. They were able to document abuses in several subcontractors to key brands: H&M; Joe Fresh (Loblaws); Marks and Spencer; and the Gap. These same companies have been the subject of a number of other stories alleging abuses, including by the Global Labor Justice organization (https://globallaborjustice.org/, accessed July 21, 2021).[5]

The Worker Rights Consortium (WRC) is an NGO that monitors and advises on workers' rights. We accessed their factory investigations page (https://www.workersrights.org/our-work/factory-investigations/, accessed July 21, 2021) to check on the leading sport shoe brands' records in terms of subcontractor abuse allegations for the period 2010–19 (Table 4.2). We also checked on the clothing brands listed just once in the above searches to see if they came up in the WRC website. See Appendix A for the full database by source.

---

5 See Hira and Benson-Rea (2017) for a discussion of the Rana Plaza Factor collapse, where several brands were present. See also https://www.globalcitizen.org/en/ content/british-retailers-exploit-child-syrian-refugees-tu/?template=next, Accessed July 21, 2021.

Table 4.2 Multiple Listings of Alleged Labor Violations by Major Apparel and Footwear Brands' Subcontractors from Primary Reporting Sources, 2010–19

Company	HQ Country	Countries of Alleged Violations & Years
Loblaw	Canada	Bangladesh (2013–17); Cambodia (2015)
Asics	Japan	Cambodia (2013); China (2014)
Uniqlo	Japan	China (2015); Indonesia (2015)
H&M	Sweden	Cambodia (2013, 2015)
Gap	US	multiple sites (2005–19)
JC Penney	US	multiple sites (2010–13)
Nike	US	multiple sites (2006–19)
WalMart	US	multiple sites (2010–19)

Source: See Appendix A.

Electronics

While there have been occasional stories in the mainstream press about labor abuse in the electronics industry, such as articles about Chinese workers for Foxconn, a leading subcontractor to Apple, committing suicide from 2010 to 2016, there has not been any systematic effort to document the industry. As with the other sectors, we consulted the BHRR website, using the sector search category of "technology, telecom, and electronics" and "death" or "killings" for 2010–19. We also consulted the GoodElectronics website (https://goodelectronics.org/, accessed July 21, 2021) which is a network of NGOs, unions, activists, and researchers dedicated to studying the industry in terms of both human rights and the environment. They receive funding from the EU. We examined their report titles (publications) from 2010 to 2019. Samsung is also the subject of a 2013 report by the Asia Monitor Resource Centre, a labor rights watchdog based in Hong Kong. IndustriAll is a global union federation operating from Copenhagen (http://www.industriall-union.org/, accessed July 21, 2021). Their website allows for a search for stories from their newsfeed by sector. Table 4.3 summarizes our findings for electronics.

Table 4.3 Multiple Listings of Alleged Labor Violations by Major Electronics Brands from Primary Reporting Sources, 2010–19

Company	HQ	Place of Alleged Violation and Years
Apple	US	China (2010–16)
Foxconn	Taiwan	China (2010–16)
Samsung	South Korea	South Korea (2013–17); Brazil (2017); India (2017); China (2012)

Source: See Appendix A.

Do Controversies Affect ESG Ratings?

Companies Named in Repeated Issues Are Mostly Covered by Newsfeeds, but in an Episodic and Haphazard Fashion

We do not seek to personally verify the labor violations claims from the data extracted in Table 4.3, since they are reported by multiple sources, including independent ones, and acknowledged by the companies themselves. Our purpose, rather, is to examine whether the serious adverse events are reflected in ESG scores. We think this is particularly the case for large multinational companies that have been mentioned repeated times and/ or been named in serious allegations involving violence. We, therefore, synthesize the following cases to check out:

(a) are they reported in Factiva, the most commonly used newsfeed by business raters, with comprehensive global coverage including some local news sources;
(b) if the adverse events reported are reflected in ESG ratings of the companies, which we tackle in the following section.

In regard to the first question, the answer is mixed. We examined our first two adverse incidents in our tables: violence and deaths reported at Rio Tinto's mines in Papua New Guinea and Mozambique from 2013 to 2014, and at Barrick's proposed Pascua Lama mine in Chile in 2001. As noted above, these were highlighted by multiple NGO sources as extremely serious, and, from an investment perspective, could (and did in all three cases) close down the mines with major financial repercussions. In short, they are incidents that should have been picked up by newswires and then reflected in ESG ratings.

We conducted Factiva searches for words in the headlines of article (all done on August 4, 2021). We started with Rio Tinto and Mozambique or New Guinea for 2001, and found 1,244 different stories, most of which were business related, such as changes in stock prices. An analyst or an artificial intelligence (AI) search engine would have been hard-pressed to find the handful of articles about the controversies around the mines. In fact, within this search, we find just five articles related to the subject "assault," or 0.4% of the articles. There were just four articles when we instead narrowed the subject matter to "corporate social responsibility." And remember, this is when we purposely reduced the subject matter to the two countries where we already know concerns happened. An AI (automated) or general analyst who did not know of these incidents would have found these five articles drowned out in other news. Simply put, the search engines behind

ESG ratings are based on quantity of articles, not seriousness of incidents, and most articles are about business, not social performance.

We did a second search for Barrick and Chile for 2001. In this initial search, 155 stories showed up. However, the vast majority were about merger plans for Barrick including the Pascua Lama mine, not the incipient controversy that would eventually lead to its closure. What about an analyst who may have heard or seen some story about the controversy around the Pascua Lama mine in 2001? When we added "Pascua Lama" to the search, we found a very short one paragraph article about Barrick's plans to begin work on the mine and plans around mergers with other companies.[6] The article says nothing about the environmental concerns around the mine by local residents. After expanding the search for the time period from 2001 to August 4, 2021, we found 1,200 unique stories around Barrick and Pascua Lama. In fact, the headlines are very positive in nature from 2001 until 2005, when headlines about concerns around glaciers close to the mine start to show up. These continue all the way through July 2021. Therefore, even if an investment analyst looked at the long-term history of Barrick, knowing about this controversy, they would not have been able to fathom the very serious implications of its initial investment decision in 2001, which have had financial repercussions for going on two decades now.

In sum, *the stories around the controversies are mostly available in the general news databases SRI investors rely upon, if one drills down to the second layer of notes around the number of controversies by category. However, the articles about them are each about a paragraph long, offering no real details or context about it and thus burying their importance.* Unless an analyst really looked into the details and circumstances under which the mines closed or the strikes ensued they could not really understand how serious the incident was. More importantly, since these events are tracked as they happen, *there is no way to track over time how the controversies evolved or the effectiveness of company actions to solve the underlying issues,* as they did, over a decade or more of developments. Thus, there would be no way to assess if the company's response was responsive and responsible, and thus to pressure the company, or reward it, for resolution of the underlying issues. In the case of Pascua Lama, an analyst would have really had to dig into the case, as we did above, to understand the challenges for the mine, and to look across Barrick operations to see that this is not an isolated incident, but part of a suite of issues around their operations. There is nothing in the rating systems that allows them to do that at this point. *It would require*

---

6 The article is "Barrick Straight onto Pascua-Lama/Veladero," *Mining Journal*, June 29, 2001, downloaded from Factiva. It is 204 words long.

them to move well beyond the ratings firms to dig into primary research, which none do at present. This helps to explain why protests and threats of expropriation are more likely to affect immediate company behavior than SRI ratings, and why the ratings fail to anticipate, monitor, or curb ESG violations.

Money Managers Get Limited and Obscured Data on Egregious Allegations through ESG Indices

If ESG controversies tend to get buried in newsfeeds and the panoply of news stories about companies' financial strategies, events, and product/brand placement, do the reporting indices adequately report such controversies so that pension fund managers can take them into account?

In this section, we examine the companies with alleged serious human rights violations from our lists above and see how they played out in companies' ESG scores. Unfortunately, most ratings firms are not only opaque on their exact methods but also very expensive to access. Most universities cannot afford it. Simon Fraser University's library only afforded us access to data from two ratings companies, Refinitiv and Bloomberg, which, nonetheless, are two of the leading reporting agencies with thousands of subscribers, including leading institutional investors. However, Bloomberg's ESG data were generally far more limited in both years covered (generally from 2018) and the number of indicators. This in and of itself is problematic for any long-term monitoring of ESG issues, so we focused on Refinitiv.

For each company, we examined the overall ESG report, as well as their overall ESG ranking in the "peer report." Peers are chosen by an algorithm that selects companies that belong to the same subsector and have a comparable market cap. The year of peer reports was not always consistent with the adverse events during the period due to reporting gaps; in those cases, we chose the peer report in the year closest to the year, or the last year, where there were multiple years, of the incidents. The peer group generally includes around 50–100 companies involved in similar product lines around and of a similar market cap.

We then looked at the time period of the reported incident(s) and traced out their effects on ESG. Table 4.4 summarizes our findings for each sector. We report the overall ESG ranking of the company compared to peers (for the year closest to the incident date); the human rights and community scores (aggregate indicators that are part of the social score); the overall social scores; the controversies grade; and the overall ESG grade. Note that some of the companies from Table 4.1 did not have data; most have been closed down or were bought out, and that the Refinitiv ESG data generally date from 2005, limiting which incidents we could cover. Also, *please note we report every year during the time period of the scandal, in order to present an accurate picture of ratings over*

Table 4.4 Refinitiv Reporting on Serious Human Rights Allegations in the Mining Sector and Resulting Category Evaluations (Over Multiple Years)

Company	HQ Country	Countries of Alleged Violations & Years	Peer Rank, ESG Score (Year)	HR Scores (Years)	Community Score (Years)	Social Score (Years)	Controversies Score (Years)	ESG Combined Score (Years)
Rio Tinto	Australia	Mozambique, Papua New Guinea (2013–14, 2017)	6(2017)	A-,B+, A+	A+ (all years)	B, A-, A-	B+, C+, C-	B+, B, B-
Oceana Gold	Australia	Philippines (2016); El Salvador (2018)	77(2019)	C+,C-	A, A-	B, B-	D+, A+	C+, C+
Vale	Brazil	Brazil (2015–2020), major tailings dam failure	5(2016)	A+ (all years)	A+ (all years exc. 2018, A-)	A (exc. 2015, A+)	D, D,-A,A, D-, D-	C+,C,A,A-, C+, C+
BHP	Australia	Brazil (2015–20, major tailings dam failure	2(2016)	A+,A+,A, A,A,A-	A, A-,A, A,A,A+	A+,A,A, A,A-,A	B,-D-,D,-, B,D,D-	B+,C+,C+, B+,C+,C+
Barrick	Canada	Tanzania, Papua New Guinea (2010–18)	12(2018)	A+ (all years)	A+(2010–12, 2018);A(2013, 2015–17); B+(2014)	A+(2010–12); A(2011–18)	D+, B+,C, D-,D,A+,B, A-,A+	B-,A-,B,C, C+,A,B+, A-,A
Fortuna Silver Minerals	Canada	Mexico (2012–18)	101(2018)	D-(2012–17), B-(2018)	B-,A,A-, B-,(2015–17), B+	D+ (2012–12, 2015–16); C-(2014); C-(2017), B(2018)	A+ all years	C-(2011–12, 2016); D+(2014), D(2015); C(2017); B-(2018)

(Continued)

Table 4.4 (*Continued*)

Company	HQ Country	Countries of Alleged Violations & Years	Peer Rank, ESG Score (Year)	HR Scores (Years)	Community Score (Years)	Social Score (Years)	Controversies Score (Years)	ESG Combined Score (Years)
Hud Bay Minerals	Canada	Guatemala (2010–17)	59(2018)	D+,D-(2012–2016); C+(2017)	A,B(2011–12); A+(2013–17)	B-,C+ (2011–12); B-(2013–16), B+(2017)	D,A+(2011–12, 2014, 2016–17), D+(2013), C(2015)	C,C+,B-, C,B,B-,B-,B+
Harmony Gold	South Africa	South Africa (2012–18)	43(2018)	A(2012–13), A-(2014); A+ (2015–18)	A,B+,B-,C+ (2015–18)	A-(all years)	D+(2012–13, 2016); D(2014, 18),A+(2015), C+(2017)	C+(2012–14), A-,B-,B,C
Anglo American	South Africa	South Africa (2013–18), silicosis/ TB case	18(2018)	A+(2013–18)	A(2013–14, 2018); A-(15); C(16); B+(17)	A,A+,A, A-(16–18)	C,A+,D+,B, A+,A	B,A,B-,B+, A-(17–18)
Anglo Gold Ashanti	South Africa	South Africa (2013–18), silicosis/ TB case	58(2018)	B-(2013–14, 17); C+(15); B(16)	A+(all years)	B+(2014–15), B(2017–18), B+(16)	D(2013, 15); A-(14),B+(16); A+(17)	C+(13,15); A-(14,16), B+(17)
Gold Fields	South Africa	South Africa (2013–18), silicosis/ TB case	14(2018)	B(2013–14); B-(15); A+ (16–18)	A-,B,A,A+ (16–18)	B+(13,15); B(14); A(16–18)	C-(13)A+ (14–17); A(18)	B-(13); B+ (14–15); A-(16–18)

Company	HQ Country	Countries of Alleged Violations & Years	Peer Rank, ESG Score (Year)	HR Scores (Years)	Community Score (Years)	Social Score (Years)	Controversies Score (Years)	ESG Combined Score (Years)
Glencore	Switzerland	Peru (2015), Philippines (2014), DRC (2012–14)	1(2016)	A-(2012); A(2013–15)	B,B+,B,B+	A-(12–14),A	D+,B+, D+,C+	C+,B+, B-B+
Vedanta Resources	UK	India (2018)	36(2018)	A-	A	A	D+	C+
Newmont	US	Peru (2005–13)	9(2016)	A-,B,B+, B(2008–12), B-(13)	B+,A,A+ (2007–13)	A-(all years)	A(05,07, 09–10,12); A+(06,08); C+(11); B+(13)	A-(05,07–10); B(06); B+(11,13); A(12)

Notes: HR = human rights scores; early years reported first; peer rank—lowest is best; no Vedanta data for after 2018; Newmont data from 2005.

Source: Refinitiv was accessed August 5, 2021.

the scandal lifetime and track their trajectory. This allows us to see if there is a lag time before the reporting of the event gets reflected in the ratings system.

The complexity of Table 4.4 speaks for itself. *A money manager would be very hard pressed to trace out corporate behavior over time, and whether it's improving, or if adverse events have really led to changes in company policies.* Simply put, the numbers do not reflect the reality. For example, *at the same time that protestors were killed in Tanzania and Papua New Guinea related to Barrick mines, it received a B+-A+ in its human rights, community, and social scores.* Indeed, in many of the sections, such as the human rights score, *the data consist of whether the company has a policy* around something like child labor (leading to a true/false entry), not around whether the policy is at all effective. The lack of valid, consistent, and reliable data sources explains the huge variation in most companies' scores from year to year. Simply put, money managers and ratings indexers are *myopic*, thinking only of the next reporting cycle, rather than looking through the decade or more of corporate behavior and if and how companies improve their reactions to scandals. This reflects the structure of corporate financial systems, which are oriented towards stock prices, not long-term performance.

Moreover, the peer rank scores do not reflect the scandals in any consistent fashion, with companies enduring serious controversies, such as Glencore and BHP being among the leaders in ESG scores. The human rights, social and community scores are, moreover, clearly inadequate, with *most companies suffering scandals still earning As or Bs* during the periods. Only Fortuna Silver and HudBay have scores reflecting the serious allegations against them. The system works somewhat better in terms of the controversies score, though even here the record during serious allegations, and often court cases, varies widely from one year to the next, going from D to A back to D again in the case of Vale, which was responsible for one of the worst mine environmental disasters in history during the period. Nor is there any clear pattern for the ESG combined score, which demonstrates equal variation and volatility. None of this should be surprising given what we have discussed earlier, namely that *the information system relies on a hit-and-miss, one-off strategy of event reporting, rather than what is needed, which is a serious on-the-ground investigation and understanding of the sector and what's happening on the ground.* We now turn to death-related incidents in the clothing and footwear sectors.

The apparel/footwear sector yields the same results (Table 4.5). *At the same time that the Rana Plaza factory collapsed in 2013,* Loblaw, H&M, the Gap, and Walmart, *all brands linked to work at the site, have positive scores.* Loblaw had an A- for controversies, and a B- overall score; H&M and the Gap were in the A/B range over the whole period. Only Walmart demonstrates some red flags with lower scores in several categories. But even here, the low grades are mixed in with some higher ones. And Walmart has a very high peer ESG ranking.

Table 4.5 Refinitiv Scores for the Clothing and Footwear Sector around Serious Human Rights Allegations and Resulting Scores

Company	HQ Country	Countries of Alleged Violations & Years	Peer Rank, ESG Score (Year)	HR Scores	Community Scores	Social Scores	Controversies Scores	ESG Combined Scores
Loblaw	Canada	Bangladesh (2013–17); Cambodia (2015)	21(2016)	C-(2013–4); D+(15); B(16–17)	B+(2013–16); C+(17)	B-(all years)	A-,A+, A,A-,A	B-,B+, B(15–17)
Asics	Japan	Cambodia (2013); China (2014)	3(2015)	B,B-	B,A-	B,B+	A+,D+	B,C
Uniqlo (Fast Fashion)	Japan	China (2015); Indonesia (2015)	36(2015)	C+	C	B	A+	B
H&M	Sweden	Cambodia (2013, 2015)	14(2016)	A+,A+	B-,A	B+,A	A,B+	B+,B+
Gap	US	Multiple sites (2005–19)	9(2019)	A(2006); A+(all other years)	A(06,08–10); A-(07); A+(all other years)	B+(05); B(06); A(07–14); A+(15–19)	A+(05–06, 08–11,13,17–19); A-(07,14); B-(12); C-(16)	B+(05,08,12); B-(06); A-(07,10, 14–15); A(09,11, 13,17–19)
Nike	US	Multiple sites (2006–19)	9(2019)	B+,B-,C+, D-(09–10); C+, C,B-,C+,B+,B, A+(17–18); A	A(06),B(07, 17–19,A+ (08–11,13–14); A-(12,15); B+(16)	B(06–7, 09–10); B+(08,12,14, 16); A-(11,13, 15,17–19)	A-,B+,C-, D(09–10); C+(11); A+; B+; C+; A+; B+; A+(17–18); D	B(06–07, 11–12,16); C(08–10,19); B+(13,17); B-(14); A-(15)
WalMart	US	Multiple sites (2010–19)	6(2019)	A(10–12); B+(14–15); B(16–17); C+(18); A+(19)	A-(10,12,14); B+(11); A(13,15–18); A+(19)	A-(10–11, 13–15,16,19); A(12); B+(17–18)	D-(10–11, 13–15,17,19); D(12); A-(16)	C(10–11, 13–15,19); C+(12,18); A-(16)

Notes: Early years reported first; peer rank—lowest is best.

Source: Refinitiv was accessed August 5, 2021.

What is a money manager to make of scores that vary widely from C/D to A from one year to the next? It would be very hard for such a person to get to the roots of the problem, to see if Walmart's behavior has really changed in response to such events. The overall lack of accountability thus gives leeway for companies to keep repeating the same behavior, with lower costs to covering them up or obscuring them through company reports or social media blitzes, to drown out any real adverse events.

What happens when things get so bad the workers commit suicide, as happened in Foxconn factories in China from 2010 to 2016, which was widely covered in the media, or when workers in one's home country claim the company created cancerous conditions, as happened with Samsung, winning a settlement? Surely such events must be reflected in ESG indices for the often egregious conditions in the electronics sector?

As Table 4.6 demonstrates, such serious events do seem to show up fairly consistently in the controversies and combined scores, but not in our other categories. In these instances, the information system seems to be offering money managers warning signs about ESG conditions, and particularly the heavy reliance on Foxconn by a large number of multinational firms. Yet, Foxconn's supply chain value must be such that their Western partners are unable to break such bonds, even despite the repeated scandals. Suicides are not enough to break contracts; one starts to provide nets for would-be jumpers. *There are no signs that such poor ratings have adversely affected these companies or changed supply chains.* On the contrary, Apple and Samsung continue to be in the top 15 of all global companies in terms of basic financial performance, from market capitalization to revenues. Clearly, *neither consumers nor pension fund managers are punishing companies for labor or environmental violations.*

Comparing Refinitiv Findings to MSCI Ratings: More of the Same

We were able to gain access to contemporary (2021) MSCI reports and notes for three of the companies of interest. Though we did find longer-term recording of controversies for the companies, the overall effect of such incidents on ESG ratings does not appear to be significantly different than Refinitiv scores. For example, *MSCI's analyst insights note that the Vice Chairman of Samsung was arrested on corruption charges in 2021, however, the company still received an overall A score in its intangible value assessment score*, which summarizes ESG risks. Under the Walmart controversies notes, nothing is mentioned about overseas labor issues. Walmart receives a BB rating, due to "multiple controversies," without explaining what they are. A similar statement explains Apple's BBB rating, "corporate behavior controversies."

Table 4.6 Refinitiv Scores for the Electronics Sector around Serious Human Rights Allegations and Category Evaluations

Company	HQ	Place of Alleged Violation and Years	Peer Rank, ESG Score (Year)	HR Scores	Community Scores	Social Scores	Controversies Scores	ESG Combined Scores
Apple	US	China (2010–16)	19(2016)	A+(10–13); B(14); C+(15–16)	B+,A+,A,B, B-(14–15),C+	B(10–12); B-(13,16); C+(14–15)	D-(10–15); D(16)	C-(10–12,14–15); C(13,16)
Foxconn	Taiwan	China (2010–16)	31(2015)	B(10),A-(11, 13–14,16); A(12,15)	C+(10,12–13); C-(11,15; C(14); D+(16)	C+(10, 12–14,16); C(11,15)	A+(10–11,15–16); D+(12); D(13–14)	D+(10,12,15–16); D(11,13–14)
Samsung	S. Korea	S. Korea (2013–17); Brazil (2017); India (2017); China (2012)	2(2017)	A+(12–13);A; A-;B+(16–17)	B+(12–13);A(14); A-15–16);A+(17)	A(12–14, 16–17)A-(14)	D(12,14);D+(13); C+(15);D-(16–17)	C+(12,14, 16–17);B-(13); B+(15)

Notes: Early years reported first; peer rank—lowest is best.
Source: Refinitiv was accessed August 5, 2021.

Summary of How Deaths Are Reflected in SRI ESG Reporting Systems

We have found numerous instances where locals have died in incidents involving Western companies over a decade of data. We then traced out whether such events were reported, and what effect they had on their ESG ratings. We found that one would largely need to be keenly aware of and interested in a particular company's ethical performance to grapple with the seriousness and response to serious human rights violations. Absent a serious investigation, the incidents are buried in positive financial news stories and in the categorial ratings. They are further buried in creating a composite score across the different categories.

There are at least five underlying flaws in the reporting system that desperately need attention:

• Unclear and contrasting definitions and measurements of CSR concepts and indicators
• Hidden ratings weightings and formulas for most of the ratings agencies
• Weak data quality and consistency—lack of primary sources; inconsistent and over-represented sources; issues with data validity and reliability
• Inability to compare easily across companies, sectors, and time
• Episodic and haphazard reporting that emphasizes avoiding extremely negative scores, which are almost always temporary, thus having no lasting penalty or incentive for improvement

In sum, what we have seen is that while serious human rights allegations are often reported in aggregate news sources and in controversies scores, the overall impact is generally buried amidst the panoply of reported indicators and contradictory and volatile scores, allowing companies and investors to simply ignore scandals involving deaths as temporary inconveniences. *Having a human rights policy in name, in this sense, counts as much as whether a human rights violation occurred. The information system has no memory, keeps no tabs on whether and how companies have responded and changed, and thus offers no clear signal on whether a company is (less) likely to be involved in egregious allegations or scandals in the future. Lacking primary data and context, the system incentivizes gaming the indicators and burying the isolated report about adverse effects, as well as drowning out any reports about serious issues and events with company reports and social media.* Perhaps most damning is the fact that there is nothing in the current reporting system oriented toward resolving the recurring issues it reports.

Chapter 5

CONCLUSION: HOW TO IMPROVE THE RATINGS SYSTEM TOWARD HARMONIZATION, TRANSPARENCY, AND ACCOUNTABILITY

We have documented how trillions of dollars are being invested in environmental, social, and governance (ESG) reporting, with little to show for them in terms of improving corporate or industry behavior or host community support for Western investment or addressing the fundamental issues around labor or human rights or environmental destruction including climate change. To be fair, it must be truly daunting for accountants who have no training in nonfinancial subjects to try to meet the incredibly detailed and often multiple reporting requirements for criteria that are often not only nonquantitative in nature, but nuanced, complex, evolving, and subjective based on differing stakeholders' perspectives, subjects that require social sciences training and methods. The current attempts to shift toward some uniformity of reporting standards as represented by the Sustainability Accounting Standards Board; to try to improve the reporting of "externalities," particularly climate change; and to focus on improving the transparency and input of activist shareholders to try to push Western companies to move past their understandable focus on short-term share prices, including using Western court systems are all positive and laudable and reflect serious ethical motivations/guidance in corporate activity as well as ratings agencies, such as Bloomberg, but are clearly falling short of addressing basic issues. Nor do they focus adequately on non-climate change issues, including human and labor rights or other forms of environmental degradation.

From the perspective of company incentives, the issues are even more daunting. As Sandberg (2013) points out, corporate social responsibility (CSR) and socially responsible investment (SRI) are fundamentally flawed in their conception. If the main measure of a company's success is profit as reflected in share price, and that of a money manager, return on investment, how can this be reconciled with ethical responsibility? Sandberg notes that there is an underlying *fiduciary responsibility* of CEOs, CFOs, and pension fund managers to maximize returns. This is incompatible with the ideas behind CSR/SRI that there are other measures of success that are equally important; certainly, *there is nothing in most shareholder or general financial assessments that would reflect anything other than financial return mattering.* The idea that CSR/SRI leads, in the long run, to a better return is at best unproven, and ignores the short-term nature of financial decision-making. Thus, the goal of CSR is to make investment decisions that avoid corporate embarrassment in the Western press, and not to adhere to any clear ethical practices or norms.

Even as we have shown that CSR and SRI reporting are based on faulty data, the lack of clear incentives means that standardizing reporting alone will not solve the problem. The current data, as demonstrated in our human rights exercise, is insufficient even for basic negative screening (avoiding major scandals), let alone embracing ethical principles as important as financial ones. Simply put, the system reflects the predominance of return on investment with lip service to ethics. Our core hope for change is that the business community will tire of wasting money on investments that are for show only. If the primary emphasis is to avoid scandal, over time, the flaws in the reporting system will become known, as has been the case with tax evasion, and window dressing will no longer be enough. *Scandals continue to happen and negatively affect financial returns over the long-run in ways that are nowhere reflected in CSR or ESG reporting systems.* Materiality comes in the long run to reveal the flaws in the system, through the millions lost by Barrick in Pascua Lama, or through Apple's 2022 inability to manage its workforce to build iPads, losing the ability to deliver products during the holiday buying season. In fact, across the world, illegal artisanal and small miners are taking matters into their own hands, to provide themselves with employment and incomes, undercutting large multinationals and host governments, and reflecting the utter failure of formal mining to improve living standards in host communities in the South. Simply put, the reporting system does not catch the problems it is purported to flag, thus its primary function of signaling risk is unfulfilled. *Until there are real consequences for major losses due to ethical violations, incentives for change will remain rhetorical.*

What Do CSR and SRI Really Mean?

At the core of the issue is the concept of CSR itself, which is simultaneously fraught and paradoxical. Essentially, it is a system that has contradictory foundations—on the one hand, suggesting that corporate and investment decisions are voluntary and should be market-driven, reflected in the "financial materiality" prerequisite for the listing of most CSR and SRI indicators. On the other hand, it is subjective in terms of dealing with complex ethical issues, not all directly negatively affecting the bottom line in the short run (such as worker or environmental exploitation) that companies need to navigate across varying situations without guidance or competencies. On top of this, the problem of externalities to corporate activities including labor, social, and environmental effects of their activities, reflects the limited ability of CSR to solve real-life problems (Brammer et al. 2012), particularly in institutional environments where basic rights and protections are not enforced.

Even a simple step toward uniform reporting as occurs in financial issues is blocked by the proprietary formulas that are the basis of the business model for CSR and SRI reporters. Lacking a clear definition or even weighting, the information environment is so complex as to seemingly be set up to obfuscate, rather than elucidate.

As Cash (2021) points out, there are multiple issues with ESG reporting:

- Lack of transparency
- Incommensurability
- No uniformity or guidelines on trade-offs among criteria
- Difficulties in interpreting aggregate scores
- No consideration of stakeholder preferences

To these, we have added:

- No primary data gathering
- Inherent conflict of interests and, sometimes, ownership between ratings agencies and respondents
- Importance of key events is lost in the noise of information
- No follow-through on company responses or rewards for long-term efforts at improvement
- No enforcement and ephemeral or nonexistent penalties for bad scores
- Inability to understand or measure on-the-ground issues, and no attempt to try to resolve them in a thoughtful way

Therefore, even where a company would want to consciously commit to CSR, the tools do not exist. A growing number of studies (Chatterji et al. 2016; Conway 2019; Gibson Brandon et al. 2021) find that there are *striking divergences among ratings firms* of their ESG assessments of companies, creating a serious problem for money managers to make portfolio assessments. "The Aggregate Confusion Project" by MIT professors (https://mitsloan.mit.edu/sustainability-initiative/aggregate-confusion-project, accessed July 28, 2021), concludes that ESG data are "noisy and unreliable." They find that while credit ratings between Moody's and Standard & Poor's are correlated at 0.92, ESG ratings for prominent agencies only correlate at 0.61. They trace the sources of the divergence to differences in both measurement (which indicators are used to measure certain attributes) and scope (which indicators are included in each of the ESG categories) (Berg et al. 2020). On top of this is serious inconsistency over time in regard to ratings methodologies, leading to highly divergent scores given to the same companies over the same time periods as the methods shift and data is changed retroactively (Berg et al. 2021). kostantonis and Serafeim's (2019) modeling efforts find four key sources for ratings divergence: data inconsistency, distortions around benchmarking, data imputation based on differing models, and inconsistency in the availability of information about companies. They provide an example in regard to the first criterion of twenty different ways that employee health and safety can be reported. In terms of benchmarking, they find serious differences in how company peer groups are constructed.

The harmonization efforts toward reporting standards in the United States and the European Union (EU) are laudable and should be encouraged. But even if they were able to create a uniform standard, it would not solve other more fundamental challenges. These include conflicts of interest whereby ratings firms are owned by investment services firms, many of whom are also investors in companies and run their own mutual funds and corporate bond and related capital-raising instruments. Dimson et al. (2020) compare major companies across three different ratings systems: FTSE Russell, Sustainalytics, and MSCI, and find striking divergences, with a correlation of just 0.45. They also cite the example of Tesla during 2018–19 which had an exemplary rating from MSCI, a middle-level one from Sustainalytics, and a low measure from FTSE. They attribute the differences to how the different raters judged emissions, with low estimates coming from including factory emissions. The authors also conclude that there is a slight penalty for ethical investment. Similarly, Dyck et al. (2019) among others, finds that the country origins of the investor matter, concluding that weaker norms in the United States mean that investors have less effect on ESG outcomes than European investors. Del Guidice and Rigamonti's (2020) study on ESG scores concludes that third-party audits can make a significant difference in terms of improving the quality of company ESG information.

If readers are still skeptical, they should consider that the "smoke and mirrors" nature of financial reporting is hardly surprising to insiders. The former CEO of MSCI, Henry Fernandez, pointed out in December 2021 that (Simpson et al. 2021):

"ordinary investors piling into such (socially responsible) funds have no idea that the ratings, and ESG overall, gauge the risk the world poses to a company, not the other way around," continuing that "I would even say many portfolio managers don't totally grasp that. Remember, they get paid. They're fiduciaries, you know. They're not as concerned about the risk to the world."

BlackRock's former chief investment officer for sustainable investment, Tariq Fancy, stated it even more bluntly (Fancy 2021):

The financial services industry is duping the American public with its pro-environment, sustainable investing practices. This multitrillion dollar arena of socially conscious investing is being presented as something it's not. In essence, Wall Street is greenwashing the economic system and, in the process, creating a deadly distraction. I should know; I was at the heart of it [...]. No matter what they tout as green investing, portfolio managers are legally bound (as well as financially incentivized) to do nothing that compromises profits. To advance real change in the environment simply doesn't yield the same return.

Nonetheless, the case can be made that a reliable reporting system would benefit companies. Solid, transparent, and accountable ESG reporting as reflected by the positive aim of harmonizing reporting standards would clearly *collectively* benefit companies over the long run. It would mitigate their risks as well as those of investors by avoiding activities that will create scandals and backlash, and instead enhance their brand reputation. It would support their business model to create reliable local and global community support for their industry and company, working hand in hand with political and regulatory support rather than avoiding or capturing it. It would help them problem solve by bringing key stakeholders to a common purpose, to ensure a level playing field and reducing the free-rider issues around the costs of improving standards. It would also offer them greater market opportunities— assuring both host governments/communities and investors.

It seems difficult to create accurate and thorough reporting standards in a manner that accountants are comfortable with, namely through simple continuous or ordinal rating scales. While there may be possible paths forward on E in terms of measurement, reflecting the Bloomberg-led efforts on climate change, S and G are currently defined largely in the eye of the beholder. G has come to mean in practice how a corporate board is composed and operates, creating openings for shareholder activists to promote change, such as greater diversity. However, the greater implications of G in terms of corruption and sectoral responsibility as a whole (as seen in the fossil fuels industry) and S in terms of responsibility to society as a whole are lost. The fog of conceptual, theoretical, and measurement ambiguity surrounds the whole field of CSR and principles for responsible investment. This is reflected in the panoply of indices and indicators leading to composite scores of ESG whose formulation is deliberately obscured. Such scores may be convenient for investment decision-making formulae, but they are hardly justifiable as reflecting the true aim of improving corporate behavior, which would require both transparency and accountability. Accountants and money managers naturally want easy numbers to plug in, but ESG tradeoffs, community relations/perceptions, and political arenas require much more nuanced, on-the-ground understanding of context, and consultation with local stakeholders. In my study of mining sites in Western Ghana, each site had its own unique constellation of issues, actors, and possible solution pathways; no number could have helped to explain or resolve them. Yet the fact is that there is no incorporation of primary on-the-ground analysis in SRI, and the CSR reporting done by consultants or NGOs who dispatch officers for two-week visits to the companies' headquarters suffer an inherent conflict of interest in receiving contracts from companies they need to report upon. NGOs, in fact, have no professional guidelines or norms to govern their reporting, or ensure thoroughness and accountability. Suffering from the continual need to raise funds, NGOs are often under-staffed and narrowly focused on their particular mission, missing training in social science research methods as their primary missions are around project delivery (e.g., new water systems). In sum, we need a new array of qualitatively trained assessors alongside accountants, ones who can do primary, on-the-ground research, to assess complex problems in their context, and derive lessons about how to solve them.

Resolving the Collective Action Problem

Beyond disagreement about what CSR means in principle or action, a lack of enforcement reflects the absence of genuine global authority. This brings us back to the principal-agent problem from the introduction, where information asymmetry and unevenness, based on self-reporting, lead to an inability to see which corporations are actually meeting their accepted greater responsibilities, let alone to try to improve and resolve emerging global issues such as climate change. *The movement toward more uniform CSR reporting standards, if successful, would be a big step forward, but would not solve the transparency, accountability, enforcement, or global governance issues.*

The current pithy green light reports from consultants ignore the depth of ESG issues on the ground, and thus reveal a system more geared toward "cya" or rhetorical CSR than a genuine effort to resolve or improve such issues through corporate activity. CSR departments are under-staffed and do well to measure criteria, such as the number of workplace accidents, but are not trained or oriented toward social sciences, nor do they employ local independent experts, all of which would be required to grapple with the full context. The under-funding of CSR and lumping of ESG into accounting matrices reveals an obvious truth—that companies are more concerned with the bottom line and essentially see ESG as a distraction from that; their behavior and investments speak much louder than their rhetorical pronouncements or advertising. *They would never accept such superficiality in their financial or subcontracts of their operations.* Even basic data that would be relatively straightforward to collect to reflect real conditions, such as community perceptions surveys and interviews with key stakeholders and ordinary citizens, or anonymous complaint lines, rarely exist. When it does exist, companies generally hire firms that rig the questions so that they will look favorable. For example, a mining company we studied did not ask about the complex issues around resettlement or water quality, instead, it asked a simple binary question of whether the mining company should continue to operate and provide tax revenues. It notably never asked whether the respondent citizen believed that the company delivered substantial community benefits, or how it could improve such. The survey firm hired also biased the sample through selective online population bias, avoiding taking a representative sample or visiting respondents in person. Such methods would be more costly than the public relations efforts of companies now, but they would significantly improve our knowledge of community perceptions (which is why companies avoid them now). While over the long-run engaging with local stakeholders could lead to stronger support and avoid the contestation and occasional violence multinationals occasionally suffer, sometimes losing huge amounts of investment, companies we spoke with behind closed doors indicated that they see dealing with stakeholders as a nuisance to be minimized, one that detracts from their core business and for which they have no competence.

A better system has to include *truly independent and competent monitors with free-flowing data from primary sources and analysis from those who understand the conditions on the ground leading to reports that have "teeth"* (enforcement ability). Such would require global public funds to set up a neutral global body, such as the World Trade Organization's dispute resolution mechanism. If corporations are serious about CSR, they should pay global taxes/ fees to governments to fund such a body. The fund should have long-term, say ten years of funding, and a neutral governance body of experts, not representatives of corporations or governments. It should conduct investigations of its own, not rely on third-party reporting. This could easily be funded from the trillions of dollars wasted in the current system. It is even more vital given the pressing nature of verifying climate change pledges and their long-term ability to respond to it, and to community protests that shut down operations, and the general deterioration of community conditions that threaten long-term collective business interests. Removing the conflicts and profit-based nature of the primary reporting system is essential to ensure its neutrality. Moreover, ESG scores have to matter. *Until there are consequences, no company will invest millions in time and effort to really resolve complex issues.* The complexity begins with the inability or unwillingness to acknowledge the weaknesses of their host institutions. The shift has to be towards improving actual conditions, not reporting on policies adopted or money spent on window-dressing efforts that become transparent soon enough.

The Governance Paradox

Underlying all this is the lack of coordination with host governments, who remain open to corruption and inability to regulate basic labor and environmental laws in the South, which are often both laxer than Western standards and not enforced (Hira 2020b). For example, Tashman et al. (2019) study ninety-three multinationals from fifteen emerging markets and find that where there are "institutional" voids in their home countries, there is much more likely to be decoupling of CSR activities from CSR rhetoric. Thus, *the relationship between multinationals and host governments tends more toward collusion rather than underlying tension that would promote accountability, what I have termed the "governance paradox" in the sense that the host government is unable or unwilling to reflect the needs of its own population.* Even where companies see the importance of gaining community trust, such as mining, the underlying assumption of companies is that local governments in the South are largely useless as partners, and thus they bypass them, creating a negative cycle of weak and declining local governance capacity. The resulting "governance paradox" means the community comes to see the company as a de facto government, responsible for providing basic public goods, from transport to education (Hira and Busumtwi-Sam 2021). Needless to say, companies have neither the resources nor the expertise to provide public services/ goods. They should instead be supporting building-up government capacity, a complex and costly task that would benefit them by providing a stable rule of law, but only in the long run. Their focus is too myopic at the moment to acknowledge such plain facts, which is why ESG reporting must play a larger role. They avoid investing in improving governance because this would disrupt their cozy relationship with corrupt and incompetent

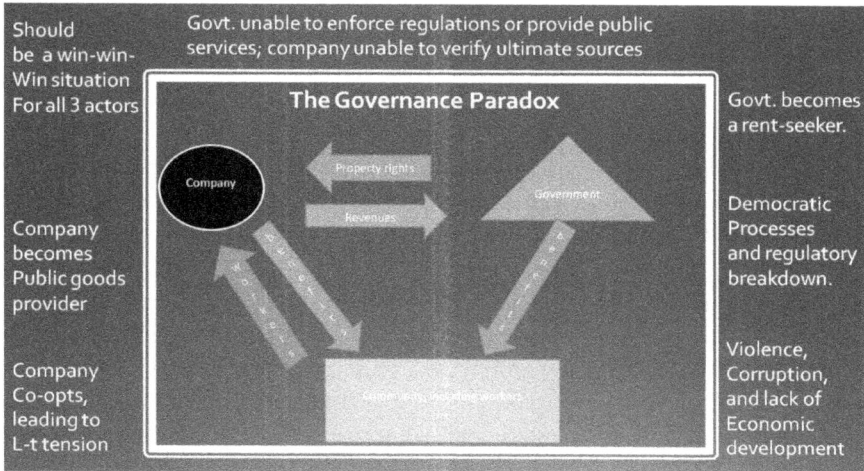

Figure 5.1 The Governance Paradox.
Source: Author.

governments and have long-term but uncertain payoffs. The Governance Paradox is illustrated in Figure 5.1.

The challenges of global reporting given the inherent regulatory weakness of many governments in the South are even more daunting. For example, one can see the challenges of screening through ethical companies who have subcontracts with unethical ones. For example, in previous work, Hira (2017) revealed that many of the issues around labor compliance in the textile industry relate to Western clothing manufacturers who ostensibly attempt to seriously engage in CSR while subcontracting out to a byzantine and ever-changing set of subcontractors who do not. Yet there is no blowback when serious violations are found. For example, major Western company chains such as Sainsbury's, Tesco, and the Gap were subcontracting to Indian factories that were engaged in child labor. Conditions were reported to the companies in 2014, and they promised to end contracts and end the use of child labor. In 2018 and again in 2021, the same violations were present upon inspection by several NGOs (Bengtsen 2018; HWW 2018; Johnson 2021). *CSR and SRI thus represent a continuation of the negative screening approach, with temporary discipline around negative incidents, and a minimum floor of behavior, rather than any push toward better outcomes. Simply put, companies are content to work with corrupt and negligent governments, hoping that selective co-optation and coercion by their partners will stifle community yearnings for development.*

Moving to a System Based on Impacts Rather than Gestures Requires Shifting Power

Our review of the methods of CSR and SRI reporting reveals a process that is reified, with *the power of information concentrated among a few actors beholden to corporate contracts, while the outcomes of the reporting,* given its muddled nature, *are largely irrelevant to decision-making. The essential approach is a defensive one, designed to demonstrate the veneer of ethical behavior to the extent necessary to assuage the money managers of pension funds.* As Richardson (2013) points out, SRI has become a technical, checkbox part of financial decision-making, an extended part of due diligence, rather than a means of transformation as envisioned by activists. As he further points out, the complex and dynamic transactions across the global economy make any true achievement of ethical behavior extremely challenging. Garsten and Jacobsson (2011) get to the heart of the matter—CSR and SRI initiatives *ignore power differentials.* They blithely recommend consensus, however, as we have seen real life conditions embody differential power among stakeholders, including access to resources, information, and influence, resulting in decision-making that reflects the most powerful, not the most vulnerable.

In sum, there are two essential issues with CSR and SRI reporting. *The first is they are largely a system of self-reporting and conflicts of interest where outside consulting firms are hired by companies to evaluate their performance.* Obviously, someone who depends for their livelihood on ongoing inspection contracts is unlikely to ask hard questions that might embarrass a company. To provide another example, I studied a mining company in Latin America that claimed 79% approval in the local region where they operated by the survey company they hired a few years ago. Upon closer inspection, I found that the survey sample was biased in coverage (not demographically representative) and by methods (using the internet or phone rather than in person), and that the questions were simplified and limited to, whether there should be mining in the region. They did not ask any questions about regional development, environmental or health conditions, or resettlement that I read about extensively in the local newspapers. My own publicly funded survey showed that public sentiment was diametrically the opposite with most citing egregious corporate behavior, and helped to explain ongoing protests at the site. This is repeated across multiple mining sites in the global South, where claims of great community relations and CSR awards persist alongside continual community protests and dissonance. In another community I visited, the mining company had won numerous global awards for CSR, yet, the roads were made of dirt and pot-holed; there was no reliable water or electricity; and a sense of desperation among all the locals we interviewed. Company officials feigned disbelief and disputed the idea that there was any "real" resentment in the community, pointing to a few high profile ribbon cutting projects, such as scholarships for a select few sons of the local elite. They stated flatly that the lack of public services was the government's problem, not theirs, while the local government stated that they received no support from either the central government or the company to improve conditions. The end result was financially material, namely a seething resentment towards the company that fed illegal local mining and threatened the company's multimillion dollar operations as well as central government revenues.

The second main issue besides lack of transparency is the *lack of any real consequences for misreporting or violations.* Activists are assuaged in the aftermath of a media scandal by ostensible measures such as breaking a contract or promising a new ethical initiative by the company. There are, simply put, no real consequences for violations or misreporting. No one is really paying attention to conditions on the ground and whether anything is improving. Simply put, those most directly affected have no voice, for a reason; their needs are problematic and complex, going beyond corporate activities to the general lack of stable or competent governance.

Companies will point to malaria campaigns and the like as evidence of their impact on the ground, which surely does make a difference in isolated instances. The fact is that there are *no* comprehensive studies demonstrating any *concrete impacts on the ground* from the millions spent annually on CSR or SRI. Guay et al. (2004) claim that NGOs influence SRI in a variety of ways: through their own mutual funds; providing advice to companies, and/ or auditing services; shareholder activism; and as activists for institutional investors. They give a few examples, such as environmental pressure on the Three Gorges Dam in China leading to Citigroup withdrawing from financing, but these are anecdotal. What we saw in examining independent news, human rights, and environmental reporting in the previous chapter is that there are still ongoing community conflicts, human rights violations, and environmental disasters occurring across the globe. So, what have CSR and SRI really changed?

Even if we accept motivated ethical principles that most in the Western corporate world say they embrace are adequate enough outside of financial return to create motivation for decision-makers to change behavior, a highly dubitable proposition (people don't enter the business world to make the world a better place), how are ethical principles defined and by whom? In the West, it was the government that stepped in to end slavery, child labor, environmental destruction; no reliance on the private sector would have improved living conditions for the workforces on which companies depend.

Even with some eventual global acceptance of human rights principles, such as the ILO labor code, different shareholders and the public at large will have different priorities. Some may prioritize women's empowerment and others environmental destruction. How would one trade-off jobs in mining or petrol versus pollution? How does one trade off the possibilities for developing local companies and employment in developing country settings, even if it means higher costs in the short term? In terms of the basic criteria, E would seem to be the most straightforward to measure and enforce, however, most environmental reporting is self-reported in the frequent absence (in the South) of capable environmental regulatory authorities and the challenges of monitoring pollution once it dissipates. Moreover, while emissions are the focus of much of the current wave of CSR/SRI activity, there are much harder environmental deterioration issues that defy easy measurement, such as loss of biodiversity or sea-level rise or ocean acidification or plastic waste. *The logic of CSR/SRI is backward in this sense, to try to note damage that has already happened by companies, rather than put in place systems to arrest it in the first place.*

In a literal sense, CSR/ESG reporting is backward, looking at past behavior over a very short period of recent history, that is quickly forgotten, as we saw in our tests in the previous chapter, rather than a deeper dive into a company/sector/country over long periods of time, to discern a pattern of behavior and mode of decision-making, or, more importantly, actual outcomes for local communities. At best it is a seriously blunt, indirect, and post hoc instrument to address serious ESG issues. Absent efforts in other arenas, particularly political and regulatory systems and civil society awareness, to help consumers make better choices, it will have very limited effectiveness in addressing root causes of such multifaceted, long-term, and deeply rooted issues. It is truly baffling that well-intentioned ESG proponents do not see the vital importance of domestic and global regulation to accomplish their goals, beginning with regulation around reporting requirements. This is the essence of the collective action problem, in that poor regulation and weak institutions are bad for business in the long run, but business can not, or has not been willing to, support regulation for its own good.

Mixed regimes have not provided any solution, though there are small victories. The many global NGOs focused on reforming corporate behavior from the Responsible Minerals Initiative to Transparency International, each with their pet cause, have good intentions and win occasional victories, such as the aforementioned attention paid to Apple after the rash of suicides in its subcontractor plants in China. However, *most NGOs* are continually searching for funding sources, and thus many *have entered into devil's bargains with companies that they are supposed to audit because the companies pay for the auditing contracts.* As Hira (2017) notes, in the Rana Plaza disaster and its aftermath, this led to a dizzying array of one-off reports and factory audits, but not real systemic change. The principal weakness is that the Bangladeshi government, like most of its counterparts in the South, is unwilling to enforce its labor and environmental laws, even though like the rest of the countries in the South, they are up to international standards. Most NGOs, after all, simply do not have the resources or competencies to monitor corporate behavior in any significant way. There are a few exceptions in limited areas, such as Amnesty International, a source of human rights abuse data used in this book. Amnesty has a solid independent funding source, and one could see an NGO contribution if there was a counterpart in environmental and social and labor reporting and much more funding for on-the-ground reporting. Similarly, more progressive ratings initiatives such as Just Capital (https://justcapital. com/) will have limited effectiveness as long as most corporations can ignore them and hide behind other ratings.

In terms of the free-rider problem, even if it didn't have direct enforcement, transparency of violations would reverberate through shame and investment implications. It requires training a professional auditing force with skills related to the sector in question and unannounced and forensic deep-dive audits of company practices. Local communities and workers need a genuine neutral party by which to voice their concerns and to hold both companies and their government partners accountable. Systematic, ongoing attention to such issues and informing consumers and institutional investors can push companies to change their practices in a way that haphazard scandal reporting could never achieve. Most important of all is to set goal posts, such as ones on diversity and local development, measured through neutral third-party verification and objective measures, just as is done with financial reporting. Last but not least, we would need to build auditing and governance capacity within host and local governments. If we could make a small fraction of CSR investments lead to real results, the progress would be palpable. Instead of seeing continual stories of labor and environmental scandals, corporations would at last begin to offer real benefits for host communities, spreading Western standards of human rights around the world in the process.

We need a new system where companies pay a general tax, as they are to the Global Compact, EITI, and GRI, to the tune of millions, that would go to an international auditing/accountability agency that has an independent board of researchers who investigate standards as well as ways to improve human rights and living conditions. The tax would need to be mandatory, using Western market access as leverage, and the standards would be made uniform. Part of the revenues would be directed to building auditing and standards compliance capacity within local governments, a far cheaper and more effective (in the long run) alternative to the international CSR regimes currently costing millions and having little to show in return. This may seem far-fetched at first glance, but it's a logical step from the sustainability and carbon border taxes presently being considered by the EU. This would, further, allow the West to compete with China, under different and better terms in regard to its investment, gaining the long-term support of host communities.

The most potent but ignored source of reform is the communities and workers themselves. In labor rights, unions are the best source of power and information for abuses by those who are directly affected. Thus, *empowering workers and communities directly through enforcing union rights*, rather than NGOs, would be a far more effective strategy. NGOs could still play a role in pressuring home (importing) Western governments to close markets off for imports associated with, and to hold companies responsible for, egregious human rights, environmental and social violations. As with the CSR system more generally, however, labor rights systems exist in most of the world in name only. NGOs and activists should be pushing for systemic reform, not focusing on winning one-off battles. There is hope. For example, the EU has proposed a carbon border tax to account for carbon emissions and sustainability standards for an array of imports. The newly renegotiated US–Mexico–Canada trade Agreement has a clause allowing for complaints if Mexico does not enforce labor rights. A viable and verifiable information system thus would be the oxygen that NGOs and activists need to breathe life into a CSR system on life support, including creating clear signals for consumers that would, combined with SRI, begin to transform corporate incentives for CSR. But in the end, it is the communities and workers in the South who need the voice, to be able to report freely on their conditions, and to pressure their own governments to enforce standards, that will be the true source of change. One simple step forward, I suggested in my reports to mining companies, is to *commission academics, paid by public global funds, to design a bona fide independent survey and stakeholder interview report of local community perceptions and priorities; metrics of community well-being; and to suggest concrete ways to improve community conditions and guide CSR revenues.* It is shocking that so few companies actually gather data on community perceptions or metrics such as access to basic services or employment, which would provide real information on whether they are genuinely making a difference in the lives of their host communities. Right now, they would rather hold a staged set of facility tours or short public meetings in which they are free to ignore, co-opt, or intimidate any brave complainers. Simply put, it would require more resources and different expertise to make a real difference in living conditions, which brings us back to the governance paradox. Companies can provide resources as they are through taxes and royalties, but they also need to pressure governments to provide public services with those monies, around a long-term economic development strategy. Thus, objective measures of progress and improvement in governance are in their long-term interests, and the only real pathway to eliminate scandals that cause them to lose money.

There is one clear force that can push for such changes, namely the rank-and-file public pensioners in the West who can push their money managers to make investment decisions that reflect and shape ethical action, not just phony reporting. Clark and Boersma (2017) cite the example of Greenpeace's 2006 campaign against Apple, calling it out for using toxic chemicals in its product lines. As consumers mobilized, the company phased out the use of two chemicals. Similarly in 2012, Greenpeace concluded a campaign pushing Apple to shift to renewable energy in its power sources, to which it agreed in 2013. Institutionalizing such efforts would allow for prolonged and sustained efforts by external agents to push companies to live up to their own CSR promises. If such efforts were focused on the reporting system, we would see a whole new horizon of social responsibility is clearly within reach. All of this could be easily accomplished for far less than the $20 billion spent annually on CSR. Corporations would at last live up to their promise and make CSR an effective investment. *Pension fund holders and activist shareholders have the power right now to make this happen, transforming the world forever.*

REFERENCES

Abbott, Kenneth W., and Duncan Snidal. 2010. 'International Regulation without International Government: Improving IO Performance through Orchestration'. *The Review of International Organizations* 5, no. 3: 315–44.

Aguinis, H. 2011. 'Organizational Responsibility: Doing Good and Doing Well'. In *APA Handbook of Industrial and Organizational Psychology* (Vol. 3), edited by S. Zedeck, 855–79. Washington, DC: American Psychological Association.

Aguinis, Herman, and Ante Glavas. 2012. 'What We Know and Don't Know About Corporate Social Responsibility: A Review and Research Agenda'. *Journal of Management* 38, no. 4: 932–68.

Akerlof, George A. 1970. 'The Market for 'Lemons': Quality Uncertainty and the Market Mechanism'. *Quarterly Journal of Economics* 84, no. 3: 488–500.

Almeida Machado, Bianca Alves, Lívia Cristina Pinto Días, and Alberto Fonseca. 2021. 'Transparency of Materiality Analysis in GRI-based Sustainability Reports'. *Corporate Social Responsibility and Environmental Management* 28, no. 2: 570–80.

Amel-Zadeh, Amir, and George Serafeim. 2018. 'Why and How Investors Use ESG Information: Evidence from a Global Survey'. *Financial Analysts Journal* 74, no. 3: 87–103.

Amer, Estefania. 2018. 'The Penalization of Non-Communicating UN Global Compact's Companies by Investors and Its Implications for This Initiative's Effectiveness'. *Business & Society* 57, no. 2: 255–91.

Anson, Mark, Ted White, and Ho Ho. 2003. 'The Shareholder Wealth Effects of CalPERS' Focus List'. *Journal of Applied Corporate Finance* 15, no. 3: 102–11.

Aouadi, A., and S. Marsat. 2018. 'Do ESG Controversies Matter for Firm Value? Evidence from International Data'. *Journal of Business Ethics* 151: 1027–47.

Asia Monitor Resource Centre. 2013. 'Labor Rights in High Tech Electronics: Case Studies of Workers' Struggles in Samsung Electronics and Its Asian Suppliers'. Hong Kong: AMRC. Found at: www.amrc.org.hk, Accessed July 21, 2021.

Awaysheh, A., R. A. Heron, T. Perry, and J. I. Wilson. 2020. 'On the Relation between Corporate Social Responsibility and Financial Performance'. *Strategic Management Journal* 41: 965–87. https://doi.org/10.1002/smj.3122.

Avetisyan, Emma, and Kai Hockerts. 2017. 'The Consolidation of the ESG Rating Industry as an Enactment of Institutional Retrogression'. *Business Strategy and the Environment* 26, no. 3: 316–30.

Badía, Guillermo, Maria C. Cortez, and Luis Ferruz. 2020. 'Socially Responsible Investing Worldwide: Do Markets Value Corporate Social Responsibility?' *Corporate Social Responsibility and Environmental Management* 27, no. 6: 2751–64.

Bae, Kee-Hong, Sadok El Ghoul, Zhaoran (Jason) Gong, and Omrane Guedhami. 2021. 'Does CSR Matter in Times of Crisis? Evidence from the COVID-19 Pandemic'. *Journal of Corporate Finance* 67: 101876, ISSN 0929-1199. https://doi.org/10.1016/j.jcorpfin.2020.101876.

Bair, J., M. Anner, and J. Blasi. 2020. 'The Political Economy of Private and Public Regulation in Post-Rana Plaza Bangladesh'. *ILR Review* 73, no. 4: 969–94.

Balkin, Jeremy K. 2016. *Investing with Impact; Why Finance is a Force for Good.* NY: Routledge.

Barkemeyer, Ralf, Lindsay Lee, and Lutz Preuss, 2015. 'On the Effectiveness of Private Transnational Governance Regimes—Evaluating Corporate Sustainability Reporting According to the Global Reporting Initiative'. *Journal of World Business* 50, no. 2: 312–25.

Barnett, M. L., I. Henriques, and B. W. Husted. 2020. 'Beyond Good Intentions: Designing CSR Initiatives for Greater Social Impact'. *Journal of Management* 46, no. 6: 937–64. https://doi.org/10.1177/0149206319900539.

Bebbington, Anthony, Elisa Arond, and Juan Luis Dammert. 2017. 'Explaining Diverse National Responses to the Extractive Industries Transparency Initiative in the Andes: What Sort of Politics Matters?' *The Extractive Industries and Society* 4, no. 4: 833–41.

Bebchuk, Lucian, and Scott Hirst. 2019. 'The Specter of the Giant Three'. *Boston University Law Review* 99: 721–41.

Belghitar, Yacine, Ephraim Clark, and Nitin Deshmukh. 2014. 'Does It Pay to be Ethical? Evidence from the FTSE4Good'. *Journal of Banking & Finance* 47: 54–62.

Belkhir, Lotfi, Sneha Bernard, and Samih Abdelgadir. 2017. 'Does GRI Reporting Impact Environmental Sustainability? A Cross-industry Analysis of CO_2 Emissions Performance between GRI-reporting and Non-reporting Companies'. *Management of Environmental Quality* 28, no. 2: 138–55.

Bénabou, Roland, and Jean Tirole. 2010. 'Individual and Corporate Social Responsibility'. *Economica* 77, no. 305: 1–19.

Bengtsen, P. 2018. 'Workers Held Captive in Indian Mills Supplying Hugo Boss. Guardian Inquiry into Concerns Raised by Hugo Boss Reveals Tamil Nadu Firm, which also Supplies Major UK Brands, Stops Women Leaving Factory'. *The Guardian.* 4 January 2018. Found at: https://www.theguardian.com/global-development/2018/jan/04/workers-held-captive-indian-mills-supplying-hugo-boss, Accessed June 3, 2021.

Berg, Florian, Kornelia Fabisik, and Zacharias Sautner. 2021. 'Rewriting History II: The (Un)Predictable Past of ESG Ratings. European Corporate Governance Institute'. Working Paper No. 708/2020. Jan. Geneva: ESGI.

Berg, Florian, Julian Kölbel, and Roberto Rigobon. 2020. 'Aggregate Confusion: The Divergence of ESG Ratings' (May 17). Found at SSRN: https://ssrn.com/abstract=3438533 or http://dx.doi.org/10.2139/ssrn.3438533, Accessed July 28, 2021.

Berliner, Daniel, and Aseem Prakash, 2015. '"Bluewashing" the Firm? Voluntary Regulations, Program Design, and Member Compliance with the United Nations Global Compact'. *Policy Studies Journal* 43, no. 1: 115–38.

Bertrand, Marianne, Matilde Bombardini, Raymond Fisman, and Francesco Trebbi. 2020. 'Tax-Exempt Lobbying: Corporate Philanthropy as a Tool for Political Influence'. *American Economic Review* 110, no. 7: 2065–102.

Bifera, Lucas. 2017. 'Titans in Energy, Finance Line Up Behind Climate Risk Disclosures'. *SNL Power Daily with Market Report.* Found at: Factiva, Accessed July 26, 2021.

Bilbao-Terol, Amelia, Mar Arenas-Parra, Verónica Cañal-Fernández, and Pablo Nguema Obam-Eyang. 2018. 'Multi-criteria Analysis of the GRI Sustainability Reports: An Application to Socially Responsible Investment'. *Journal of the Operational Research Society* 69, no. 10: 1576–98.

Bocken, N. M. P., S. W. Short, P. Rana, and S. Evans. 2014. 'A Literature and Practice Review to Develop Sustainable Business Model Archetypes'. *Journal of Cleaner Production* 65: 42–56.

Boffo, R., and R. Patalano. 2020. ESG Investing: Practices, Progress and Challenges. OECD Paris, www.oecd.org/finance/ESG-Investing-Practices-Progress-and-Challenges.pdf.

Boiral, Olivier, David Talbot, and Marie-Christine Brotherton. 2020. 'Measuring Sustainability Risks: A Rational Myth?' *Business Strategy and the Environment* 29, no. 6: 257–71.

Boiral, O., I. Heras-Saizarbitoria, M. C. Brotherton, *et al.* 2019. 'Ethical Issues in the Assurance of Sustainability Reports: Perspectives from Assurance Providers'. *Journal of Business Ethics* 159: 1111–25.

Boiral, Olivier, and Jean-François Henri. 2015. 'Is Sustainability Performance Comparable? A Study of GRI Reports of Mining Organizations'. *Business & Society* 56, no. 2: 283–317.

Boiral, O. 2013. 'Sustainability Reports as Simulacra? A Counter-account of A and A+ GRI Reports'. *Accounting, Auditing & Accountability Journal* 26, no. 7: 1036–71.

Boyer, Robert. 2005. 'How and Why Capitalisms Differ'. *Economy and Society* 34, no. 4: 509–57.

Boyer, Robert, and Yves Saillard. 2001. *Regulation Theory: The State of the Art*. London: Routledge.

Brammer, Stephen, Gregory Jackson, and Dirk Matten. 2012. 'Corporate Social Responsibility and Institutional Theory: New Perspectives on Private Governance'. *Socio-Economic Review* 10, no. 1: 3–28.

Brill, J. A., and A. Reder. 1993. *Investing from the Heart—The Guide to Socially Responsible Investments and Money Management*. NY: Crown Publishers.

Brooks, Chris, and Ioannis Oikonomou. 2018. 'The Effects of Environmental, Social and Governance Disclosures and Performance on Firm Value: A Review of the Literature in Accounting and Finance'. *The British Accounting Review* 50, no. 1: 1–15, ISSN 0890-8389. https://doi.org/10.1016/j.bar.2017.11.005.

Bruno, M., and V. Lagasio. 2021. 'An Overview of the European Policies on ESG in the Banking Sector'. *Sustainability* 13, no. 22: 12641. https://doi.org/10.3390/su132212641.

Brzeszczyński, J., B. Ghimire, T. Jamasb, and G. McIntosh. 2019. 'Socially Responsible Investment and Market Performance: The Case of Energy and Resource Companies'. *The Energy Journal* 40: 5.

Busch, Danny. 2021. 'Sustainability Disclosure in the EU Financial Sector'. In *Sustainable Finance in Europe*, by *EBI Studies in Banking and Capital Markets Law*, edited by D. Busch, G. Ferrarini, and S. Grünewald. Cham: Palgrave Macmillan. https://doi.org/10.1007/978-3-030-71834-3_12.

Capelle-Blancard, Gunther, and Stéphanie Monjon. 2014. 'The Performance of Socially Responsible Funds: Does the Screening Process Matter?' *European Financial Management* 20, no. 3: 494–520.

Carroll, A. B. 2021. 'Corporate Social Responsibility: Perspectives on the CSR Construct's Development and Future'. *Business & Society* 60, no. 6: 1258–78. https://doi.org/10.1177/00076503211001765.

Carroll, Archie B. 2015. 'Corporate Social Responsibility: The Centerpiece of Competing and Complementary Frameworks'. *Organizational Dynamics* 44, no. 2: 87–96.

Carroll, Archie B. 1991. 'The Pyramid of Corporate Social Responsibility: Toward the Moral Management of Organizational Stakeholders'. *Business Horizons* 34, no. 4, 39–48.

Carroll, Archie B., and Kareem M. Shabana. 2010. 'The Business Case for Corporate Social Responsibility: A Review of Concepts, Research and Practice'. *International Journal of Management Reviews* 2010: 85–104.

Cash, Daniel. 2021. *Sustainability Rating Agencies vs. Credit Rating Agencies: The Battle to Serve the Mainstream.* Cham, Switzerland: Palgrave Macmillan.

Cashore, B., G. Auld, and D. Newsom. 2004. *Governing Through Markets: Forest Certification and the Emergence of Non-State Authority.* New Haven: Yale University Press.

Chan, Jenny, Ngai Pun, and Mark Selden. 2013. 'The Politics of Global Production: Apple, Foxconn and China's New Working Class'. *New Technology, Work and Employment* 28, no. 2: 100–15.

Charlo, Maria J., Ismael Moya, and Ana M. Muñoz. 2015. 'Sustainable Development and Corporate Financial Performance: A Study Based on the FTSE4Good IBEX Index'. *Business Strategy and the Environment* 24, no. 4: 277–88.

Chatterji, Aaron K., Rodolphe Durand, David I. Levine, and Samuel Touboul. 2016. 'Do Ratings of Firms Converge? Implications for Managers, Investors and Strategy Researchers'. *Strategic Management Journal* 37, no. 8: 1597–614.

Chatterji, Aaron K., David I. Levine, and Michael W. Toffel. 2009. 'How Well Do Social Ratings Actually Measure Corporate Social Responsibility?' *Journal of Economics & Management Strategy* 18, no. 1: 125–69.

Clarke, T., and M. Boersma. 2017. 'The Governance of Global Value Chains: Unresolved Human Rights, Environmental and Ethical Dilemmas in the Apple Supply Chain'. *Journal of Business Ethics* 143: 111–31.

Coase, Ronald H. 1960. 'The Problem of Social Cost'. *Journal of Law and Economics* 3, no. 1: 1–44.

Collison, D., G. Cobb, D. Power., and L. Stevenson. 2009. 'FTSE4Good: Exploring Its Implications for Corporate Conduct'. *Accounting, Auditing & Accountability Journal* 22, no. 1: 35–58.

Conway, Elaine. 2019. 'To Agree or Disagree? An Analysis of CSR Ratings Firms'. *Social and Environmental Accountability Journal* 39, no. 3: 152–77.

Corrigan, Caitlin C. 2017. 'The Effects of Increased Revenue Transparency in the Extractives Sector: The Case of the Extractive Industries Transparency Initiative'. *The Extractive Industries and Society* 4, no. 4: 779–87.

Cortez, Mauricio y Antoine Maillet. 2018. 'Trayectoria multinivel de una coalición promotora e incidencia en la agenda política nacional. El caso del conflicto de Pascua Lama y la ley de glaciares en Chile'. *Colombia Internacional* 94: 3–25.

Cortez, M. C., F. Silva, and N. Areal. 2012. 'Socially Responsible Investing in the Global Market: The Performance of US and European Funds'. *The International Journal of Finance and Economicsnt* 17: 254–71.

Curran, M. Martin, and Dominic Moran. 2007. 'Impact of the FTSE4Good Index on Firm Price: An Event Study'. *Journal of Environmental Management* 82, no. 4: 529–37.

Dahlsrud, A. 2006. 'How Corporate Social Responsibility Is Defined: An Analysis of 37 Definitions'. *Corporate Social Responsibility and Environmental Management* 15: 1–13.

David-Barrett, Elizabeth, and Ken Okamura. 2016. 'Norm Diffusion and Reputation: The Rise of the Extractive Industries Transparency Initiative'. *Governance* 29, no. 2: 227–46.

Davis, K. 1973. 'The Case for and Against Business Assumption of Social Responsibilities'. *Academy of Management Journal* 16: 312–22.

Delmas, Magali A., and Vanessa Cuerel Burbano. 2011. 'The Drivers of Greenwashing'. *California Management Review* 54, no. 1: 65–87.

DiMaggio, Paul J., and Walter W. Powell. 1983. 'The Iron Cage Revisited: Institutional Isomorphism and Collective Rationality in Organizational Fields'. *American Sociological Review* 48, no. 2: 147–60.

Dimson, Elroy, Pual Marsh, and Mike Staunton. 2020. 'Divergent ESG Ratings'. *The Journal of Portfolio Management* 47, no. 1: 75–87.

Diouf, D., and O. Boiral. 2017. 'The Quality of Sustainability Reports and Impression Management: A Stakeholder Perspective'. *Accounting, Auditing & Accountability Journal* 30, no. 3: 643–67.

Doane, Deborah. 2005. 'Beyond Corporate Social Responsibility: Minnows, Mammoths and Markets'. *Futures* 37, no. 2/3: 215–29.

Drempetic, S., C. Klein, and B. Zwergel. 2020. 'The Influence of Firm Size on the ESG Score: Corporate Sustainability Ratings under Review'. *Journal of Business Ethics* 167: 333–60.

Dyck, Alexander, Karl V. Lins, Lukas Roth, and Hannes F. Wagner. 2019. 'Do Institutional Investors Drive Corporate Social Responsibility? International Evidence'. *Journal of Financial Economics* 131: 693–714.

Eccles, Robert G., Linda-Eling Lee, and Judith C. Stroehle. 2020. 'The Social Origins of ESG: An Analysis of Innovest and KLD'. *Organization and Environment* 33, no. 4: 575–96.

Eccles, Robert G., and Aldo Sesia. 2009. 'CalPERS' Emerging Equity Markets Principles'. *Harvard Business School Case Collection*. Case 409–054. Found at: https://www.hbs.edu/faculty/Pages/item.aspx?num=37077, Accessed June 21, 2021.

EITI (Extractive Industries Transparency Initiative). Website. Found at: https://eiti.org/, Accessed June 14, 2021.

———. *Key performance indicators: Measuring the impact of the EITI*. Oslo: EITI.

Ejiogu, Amanze, Chibuzo Ejiogu, and Ambisisi Ambituuni. 2019. 'The Dark Side of Transparency: Does the Nigeria Extractive Industries Transparency Initiative Help or Hinder Accountability and Corruption Control?' *The British Accounting Review* 51, no. 5: 100811.

Engineering & Mining Journal. 2020. 'Barrick Accepts Closure of Pascua-Lama Project'. *Engineering & Mining Journal* 221, no. 10: 4–5.

Escrig-Olmedo, E., María Ángeles Fernández-Izquierdo, I. Ferrero-Ferrero, J. Rivera-Lirio, and María Jesús Muñoz-Torres. 2019. 'Rating the Raters: Evaluating How ESG Rating Agencies Integrate Sustainability Principles'. *Sustainability* 11, no. 3: 915.

Farrell, Henry, and Abraham L. Newman. 2010. 'Making Global Markets: Historical Institutionalism in International Political Economy'. *Review of International Political Economy* 17, no. 4: 609–38.

Finley, Allysia. 2020. 'Bloomberg Sells "Sustainability," but Buyer Beware; Virtue-signaling Corporate Standards may be Better for Financial Firms than They Are for Investors'. *The Wall Street Journal*. March 2. Found through Factiva News Source, Accessed July 25, 2021.

Fligstein, N. 1991. 'The Structural Transformation of American Industry: An Institutional Account of the Causes of Diversification in the Largest Firms, 1919–1979'. In *The New Institutionalism in Organizational Analysis*, edited by W. W. Powell and P. J. DiMaggio, 311–36. Chicago, IL: University of Chicago Press.

Freeman, R. E. (1984). *Strategic Management: A Stakeholder Perspective*. Englewood Cliffs, NJ: Prentice Hall.

Friede, Gunnar, Timo Busch, and Alexander Basen. 2015. 'ESG and Financial Performance: Aggregated Evidence from More than 200 Empirical Studies'. *Journal of Sustainable Finance & Investment* 5, no. 4: 210–33.

Friedman, M. 1970. 'A Friedman Doctrine—The Social Responsibility of Business Is to Increase Its Profits'. *The New York Times*. Found at: https://www.nytimes.com/1970/09/13/archives/a-friedman-doctrine-the-social-responsibility-of-business-is-to.html, Accessed December 2, 2021.

———. 1962. *Capitalism and Freedom*. Chicago: University of Chicago Press.

Furstenberg, Saipira. 2018. 'State Responses to Reputational Concerns: The Case of the Extractive Industries Transparency Initiative in Kazakhstan'. *Central Asian Survey* 37, no. 2: 286–304.

Garsten, Christina, and Kerstin Jacobsson. 2011. 'Transparency and Legibility in International Institutions: The UN Global Compact and Post-political Global Ethics'. *Social Anthropology* 19, no. 4: 278–93.

Gibson Brandon, Rajna, Philipp Krueger, and Peter S. Schmidt. 2021. 'ESG Rating Disagreement and Stock Returns. European Corporate Governance Institute'. Finance Working Paper No. 651/2020. Geneva: Swiss Finance Institute.

Gillan, Stuart L., Andrew Koch, and Laura T. Starks. 2021. 'Firms and Social Responsibility: A Review of ESG and CSR Research in Corporate Finance'. *Journal of Corporate Finance* 66: 101889, ISSN 0929-1199. https://doi.org/10.1016/j.jcorpfin.2021.101889.

Gimenez, Cristina, Vicenta Sierra, and Juan Rodon. 2012. 'Sustainable Operations: Their Impact on the Triple Bottom Line'. *International Journal of Production Economics* 140, no. 1: 149–59.

Grant, Ruth W., and Robert Keohane. 2005. 'Accountability and Abuses of Power in World Politics'. *American Political Science Review* 99, no. 1: 29–43.

Del Guidice, Alfonso, and Silvia Rigamonti. 2020. 'Does Audit Improve the Quality of ESG Scores? Evidence from Corporate Misconduct'. *Sustainability* 12: 5670–86.

Egels-Zandén, Niklas, and Henrik Lindholm. 2015. 'Do Codes of Conduct Improve Worker Rights in Supply Chains? A Study of Fair Wear Foundation'. *Journal of Cleaner Production* 107, no. 16: 31–50.

ETI (Ethical Trading Initiative). Website. https://www.ethicaltrade.org/.

Fancy, Tariq. 2021. 'Financial World Greenwashing the Public with Deadly Distraction in Sustainable Investing Practices'. *USA Today*. March 16. Found at: https://www.usatoday.com/story/opinion/2021/03/16/wall-street-esg-sustainable-investing-greenwashing-column/6948923002/, Accessed December 21, 2021.

Friedman, Milton. 1970. 'A Friedman Doctrine—The Social Responsibility of Business Is to Increase Its Profits'. *The New York Times*. September 13. Found at: https://www.nytimes.com/1970/09/13/archives/a-friedman-doctrine-the-social-responsibility-of-business-is-to.html, Accessed November 16, 2021.

GIZ (German Cooperation Agency). Bonn. 'Assessing the Effectiveness and Impact of the Extractive Industries Transparency Initiative'. 2016: GIZ.

Green, Jessica F., and Graeme Auld. 2017. 'Unbundling the Regime Complex: The Effects of Private Authority'. *Transnational Environmental Law* 6, no. 2: 259–84.

GRI (Global Reporting Initiative). no date. Website. Found at: https://www.globalreporting.org/, Accessed June 11, 2021.

Guay, Terrence, Jonathan P. Doh, and Graham Sinclair. 2004. 'Non-governmental Organizations, Shareholder Activism, and Socially Responsible Investments: Ethical, Strategic, and Governance Implications'. *Journal of Business Ethics* 52: 125–39.

Gutsche, Gunnar, Anja Köbrich León, and Andreas Ziegler. 2019. 'On the Relevance of Contextual Factors for Socially Responsible Investments: An Econometric Analysis'. *Oxford Economic Papers* 71, no. 3: 756–76.

Guo, L., S.-H. Hsu, A. Holton, and S. H. Jeong. 2012. 'A Case Study of the Foxconn Suicides: An International Perspective to Framing the Sweatshop Issue'. *International Communication Gazette* 74, no. 5: 484–503.

Hall, Peter A., and Daniel W. Gingerich. 2009. 'Varieties of Capitalism and Institutional Complementarities in the Political Economy: An Empirical Analysis'. *British Journal of Political Science* 39: 449–82.

Haslam, Paul Alexander, and Julieta Godfrid. 2020. 'Activists and Regulatory Politics: Institutional Opportunities, Information, and the Activation of Environmental Regulation'. *The Extractive Industries and Society* 7, no. 3: 1077–85.

Haslam, Paul Alexander. 2018. 'The Two Sides of Pascua Lama: Social Protest, Institutional Responses, and Feedback Loops'. *European Review of Latin American and Caribbean Studies* 106: 157–82.

Haufler, V. 1999. 'Self-regulation and Business Norms: Political Risk, Political Activism'. In *Private Authority & International Affairs*, edited by C. Cutler, V. Haufler, and T. Porter, 199–223. Albany: State University of NY Press.

Hawn, O., A. K. Chatterji, and W. Mitchell. 2018. 'Do Investors Actually Value Sustainability? New Evidence from Investor Reactions to the Dow Jones Sustainability Index (DJSI)'. *Strategic Management Journal* 39: 949–76. https://doi.org/10.1002/smj.2752.

Hebb, Tessa, James P. Hawley, Andreas G. F. Hoepner, Agnes L. Neher, and David Wood, eds. 2015. *The Routledge Handbook of Responsible Investment*. NY: Routledge.

Hemingway, Christine A., and Patrick W. Maclagan. 2004. 'Managers' Personal Values as Drivers of Corporate Social Responsibility'. *Journal of Business Ethics* 50: 33–44.

Hira, Anil. 2020a. 'The Hollow Core: Breakdowns in Global Governance of CSR'. *Global Affairs* 6, no. 4–5: 461–79.

———. 2020b. 'Developing State Capacity: The Missing Variable for Corporate Social Responsibility?' *Journal of Developing Societies* 36, no. 3: 290–311.

———. 2019. *The Great Disruption: Explaining the Forces behind Trump, Brexit and LePen*. NY: Peter Lang.

———. 2017. 'Threads of Despair: An Argument for the Public Option in the Garment Industry'. In *Shirt off Your Back: Governance Reforms in the Apparel Industry after Rana Plaza*, edited by A. Hira and M. Benson-Rea, 29–80. NY: Palgrave Macmillan.

———. 2013. 'Irrational Exuberance: An Evolutionary Perspective on the Underlying Causes of the Financial Crisis'. *Intereconomics: Review of European Economic Policy* 48, no. 2: 116–23.

———. 2007. 'Time for a Global Welfare System?' *The Futurist*. May–June 2007: 27–32.

Hira, Andy, and James Busumtwi-Sam. 2021. 'Improving Mining Community Benefits through Better Monitoring and Evaluation'. *Resources Policy* 73: 102138, ISSN 0301-4207. https://doi.org/10.1016/j.resourpol.2021.102138.

Hira, Anil, Brian Murata, and Shea Monson. 2019. 'Regulatory Mayhem in Offshore Finance: What the Panama Papers Reveal'. In *The Failure of Financial Regulation: Why a Major Crisis Could Happen Again*, edited by Anil Hira, Norbert Gaillard, and Theodore H. Cohn, 191–232. NY: Palgrave Macmillan.

Hira, Anil, and Jared Ferrie. 2006. 'Fair Trade: Three Key Challenges for Reaching the Mainstream'. *Journal of Business Ethics* 63, no. 3: 107–18.

Hira, Ron, and Anil Hira. 2005. *Outsourcing America: What's Behind Our National Crisis and How We Can Reclaim American Jobs*. NY: Amacom.

Hoinathy, Remadji, and Babett Jánszky. 2017. 'The Extractive Industries Transparency Initiative (EITI): The Latest Attempt at Governing the Extractive Industries in Chad'. *The Extractive Industries and Society* 4, no. 4: 825–32.

Homeworkers Worldwide (HWW), India Committee of the Netherlands (ICN), and Centre for Research on Multinational Corporations (SOMO). 2018. 'Case Closed, Problems Persist: Grievance Mechanisms of ETI and SAI Fail to Benefit Young Women and Girls in the South Indian Textile Industry'. Amsterdam: HWW, ICN and Somo.

Hong, H., and M. Kacperczyk. 2009. 'The Price of Sin: The Effects of Social Norms on Markets'. *Journal of Financial Economics* 93, no. 1: 15–36.

Hoobler, J. M., C. R. Masterson, S. M. Nkomo, and E. J. Michel. 2018. 'The Business Case for Women Leaders: Meta-Analysis, Research Critique, and Path Forward'. *Journal of Management* 44, no. 6: 2473–99.

Human Rights Watch. 2015. '"Work Faster or Get Out:" Labor Rights Abuses in Cambodia's Garment Industry'. San Francisco: HRW. Found at: www.hrw.org, Accessed July 21, 2021.

Husted, B. 2015. 'Corporate Social Responsibility Practice from 1800–1914: Past Initiatives and Current Debates'. *Business Ethics Quarterly* 25, no. 1: 125–41.

Husted, Bryan W., and David B. Allen, 2006. 'Corporate Social Responsibility in the Multinational Enterprise: Strategic and Institutional Approaches'. *Journal of International Business Studies* 37, no. 6: 838–49.

Islam, M. A., C. Deegan, and R. Gray. 2018. 'Social Compliance Audits and Multinational Company Supply Chain: Evidence from a Study of the Rituals of Social Audits'. *Accounting and Business Research* 48, no. 2: 190–224.

Jacobs, Brian W. and Vinod R. Singhal. 2017. The Effect of the Rana Plaza Disaster on Shareholder Wealth of Retailers: Implications for Sourcing Strategies and Supply Chain Governance, *Journal of Operations Management*. 49–51: 52–66.

Jacobs, Michael, and Mariana Mazzucato, eds. 2016. *Rethinking Capitalism: Economics and Policy for Sustainable and Inclusive Growth*. NY: Wiley-Blackwell.

Jaffe, Adam B., Richard G. Newell, and Robert N. Stavins, 2005. 'A Tale of Two Market Failures: Technology and Environmental Policy'. *Ecological Economics* 54, no. 2–3: 164–74.

Jensen, Jennifer. 2019. Dam Bursts at Vale's Feijão Mine. *Engineering & Mining Journal* 220, no. 2: 4–5.

Johnson, Sarah. 2021. 'Tesco and Next among Brands Linked to Labor Abuses in India Spinning Mills'. *The Guardian*. May 28, 2021. Found at: https://www. theguardian.com/global-development/2021/may/27/tesco-admits-to-finds-evidence-of-labor-abuses-in-india-supply-chain, Accessed June 3, 2021.

Joseph, George. 2012. 'Ambiguous but Tethered: An Accounting Basis for Sustainability Reporting'. *Critical Perspectives on Accounting* 23, no. 2: 93–106.

Kang, Nahee, and Jeremy Moon. 2012. 'Institutional Complementarity between Corporate Governance and Corporate Social Responsibility: A Comparative Institutional Analysis of Three Capitalisms'. *Socio-Economic Review* 10, no. 1: 85–108.

Kanter, R.M. 1999. From Spare Change to Real Change. *Harvard Business Review* 77 (3): 122–132.

Kasekende, Elizabeth, Charles Abuka, and Mare Sarr. 2016. 'Extractive Industries and Corruption: Investigating the Effectiveness of EITI as a Scrutiny Mechanism'. *Resources Policy* 48: 117–28.

Keck, Margaret E., and Kathryn Sikkink. 2014. *Activists beyond Borders: Advocacy Networks in International Politics*. Ithaca: Cornell University Press.

Kim, Sora. 2019. 'The Process Model of Corporate Social Responsibility (CSR) Communication: CSR Communication and Its Relationship with Consumers' CSR Knowledge, Trust, and Corporate Reputation Perception'. *Journal of Business Ethics* 154: 1143–59.

Kirton, John J., and Michael J. Trebilcock. 2004. 'Introduction: Hard Choices and Soft Law in Sustainable Global Governance'. In *Hard Choices, Soft Law: Voluntary Standards in Global Trade, Environment and Social Governance*, edited by J. J. Kirton and M. J. Trebilcock, 3–32. Burlington, VT: Ashgate.

Klein, Asmara. 2017. 'Pioneering Extractive Sector Transparency. A PWYP Perspective on 15 Years of EITI'. *The Extractive Industries and Society* 4, no. 4: 771–74.

Knoll, Michael S. 2002. 'Ethical Screening in Modern Financial Markets: The Conflicting Claims Underlying Socially Responsible Investment'. *The Business Lawyer* 57, no. 2: 681–726.

Knox, Simon, Stan Maklan, and Paul French. 2005. Corporate Social Responsibility: Exploring Stakeholder Relationships and Programme Reporting across Leading FTSE Companies. *Journal of Business Ethics*. 61: 7–28.

Koenig-Archibugi, Mathias, and Kate Macdonald. 2017. 'The Role of Beneficiaries in Transnational Regulatory Processes'. *The ANNALS of the American Academy of Political and Social Science* 670, no. 1: 36–57.

Kostantonis, Sakis, and George Serafeim. 2019. 'Four Things No One Will Tell You About ESG Data'. *Journal of Applied Corporate Finance* 31, no. 2: 50–58.

KPMG. 2020. *The Time Has Come: The KPMG Survey of Sustainability Reporting: Executive Summary*. KPMG IMPACT. Found at: www.home.kpmg/sustainability reporting, Accessed December 2, 2021.

———. 2017. *The KPMG Survey of Corporate Social Responsibility Reporting 2017*. Found at: www.kpmg.com/crreporting

Krasner, Stephen D. 1983. 'Structural Causes and Regime Consequences: Regimes as Intervening Variables'. In *International Regimes*, edited by Stephen D. Krasner., 1–22. Ithaca, NY: Cornell University Press.

Kraus, Sascha, Shafique Ur Rehman, and F. Javier Sendra García. 2020. 'Corporate Social Responsibility and Environmental Performance: The Mediating Role of Environmental Strategy and Green Innovation'. *Technological Forecasting and Social Change* 160: 120262, ISSN 0040-1625.

Lane, Christel, and Jocelyn Probert. 2009. *National Capitalisms, Global Production Networks: Fashioning the Value Chain in the UK, USA, and Germany*. NY: Oxford University Press.

Lee, Yimou. 2022. 'Foxconn Unrest Risks iPhone Shipments, Weighs on Apple Shares'. *Reuters*. Found at: https://www.reuters.com/technology/more-than-20000-new-hires-have-left-apple-supplier-foxconns-zhengzhou-plant-2022-11-25/, Accessed December 14, 2022.

Levi, Margaret. 1989. *Of Rule and Revenue*. Berkeley: University of California Press.

Levitt, T. 1958. 'The Dangers of Social Responsibility'. *Harvard Business Review* 36: 41–50.

Li, Jun, and Di (Andrew) Wu. 2020. 'Do Corporate Social Responsibility Engagements Lead to Real Environmental, Social, and Governance Impact?' *Management Science* 66, no. 6: 2564–88.

Locke, Richard M. 2013. *The Promise and Limits of Private Power: Promoting Labor Standards in a Global Economy*. NY: Cambridge University Press.

López-Cazar, Ibeth, Elissaios Papyrakis, and Lorenzo Pellegrini. 2021. 'The Extractive Industries Transparency Initiative (EITI) and Corruption in Latin America: Evidence from Colombia, Guatemala, Honduras, Peru, and Trinidad and Tobago'. *Resources Policy* 70: 101907, 1–24.

López, M. Victoria, Arminda García, and Lazaro Rodriguez. 2007. 'Sustainable Development and Corporate Performance: A Study Based on the Dow Jones Sustainability Index'. *Journal of Business Ethics* 75: 285–300.

Lozano, Rodrigo. 2013. 'Sustainability Inter-linkages in Reporting Vindicated: A Study of European Companies'. *Journal of Cleaner Production* 51: 57–65.

Lüthje, Boy, and Florian Butollo. 2017. 'Why the Foxconn Model Does Not Die: Production Networks and Labor Relations in the IT Industry in South China'. *Globalizations* 14, no. 2: 216–31.

Luo, Xueming, and C. B. Bhattacharya. 2006. 'Corporate Social Responsibility, Customer Satisfaction, and Market Value'. *Journal of Marketing* 70, no. 4: 1–18.

Mackenzie, Craig, William Rees, and Tatian Rodionova. 2013. 'Do Responsible Investment Indices Improve Corporate Social Responsibility? FTSE4Good's Impact on Environmental Management'. *Corporate Governance* 21, no. 5: 495–512.

Madhav, Roopa. 2012. 'Corporate Codes of Conduct in the Garment Sector in Bangalore'. In *Challenging the Legal Boundaries of Work Regulation*, edited by Judy Fudge, Shae McCrystal, and Kamala Sankaran, 267–84. Portland, Oregon: Hart.

Maher, Rajiv, Francisco Valenzuela, and Steffen Böhm. 2019. 'The Enduring State: An Analysis of Governance-making in Three Mining Conflicts'. *Organization Studies* 40, no. 8: 1169–91.

Maignan, Isabelle, O. C. Ferrell, G. Tomas, and M. Hult. 1999. 'Corporate Citizenship: Cultural Antecedents and Business Benefits'. *Journal of the Academy of Marketing Science* 27, no. 4: 455–69.

Malden, Alexander. 2017. 'A Safer Bet? Evaluating the Effects of the Extractive Industries Transparency Initiative on Mineral Investment Climate Attractiveness'. *The Extractive Industries and Society* 4, no. 4: 788–94.

Markovic, S., O. Iglesias, J. J. Singh, *et al.* 2018. 'How does the Perceived Ethicality of Corporate Services Brands Influence Loyalty and Positive Word-of-Mouth? Analyzing the Roles of Empathy, Affective Commitment, and Perceived Quality'. *Journal of Business Ethics* 148: 721–40.

Marquis, Christopher, and Cuili Qian. 2014. 'Corporate Social Responsibility Reporting in China: Symbol or Substance?' *Organization Science* 25, no. 1: 127–48.

McCahery, Joseph A., Zacharias Sautner, and Laura T. Starks. 2016. 'Behind the Scenes: The Corporate Governance Preferences of Institutional Investors'. *The Journal of Finance* LXXI, no. 6: 2905–32.

McIntosh, Malcolm, Sandra Waddock, Georg Kell, and Kofi Annan. 2004. *Learning to Talk: Corporate Citizenship and the Development of the UN Global Compact*. NY: Taylor and Francis.

McWilliams, A., and Siegel, D. 2000. 'Corporate Social Responsibility and Financial Performance: Correlation or Misspecification?' *Strategic Management Journal* 21: 603–9.

Mellow, Craig. 2018. 'Sustainability in Search of Metrics'. *Global Finance*. April 14–17.

Mirvis, Philip, and Bradley Googins. 2006. 'Stages of Corporate Citizenship'. *California Review of Management* 48, no. 2: 104–26.

Mohr, Lois A., Deborah J. Webb, and Katherine Harris. 2001. 'Do Consumers Expect Companies to be Socially Responsible? The Impact of Corporate Social Responsibility on Buying Behavior'. *The Journal of Consumer Affairs* 35, no. 1: 45–72.

Moneva, José M., Pablo Archel, and Carmen Correa. 2019. 'GRI and the Camouflaging of Corporate Unsustainability'. *Accounting Forum* 30, no. 20: 121–37.

Moran, Theodore H. 1978. 'Multinational Corporations and Dependency: A Dialogue for Dependentistas and Non-dependentistas'. *International Organization* 32, no. 1: 79–100.

MSIntegrity. 'Not Fit-for-Purpose: The Grand Experiment of Multi-Stakeholder Initiatives in Corporate Accountability, Human Rights and Global Governance'. Found at: https://www.msi-integrity.org/not-fit-for-purpose/, Accessed June 3, 2021.

Muller, Alan, and Ans Kolk. 2010. 'Extrinsic and Intrinsic Drivers of Corporate Social Performance: Evidence from Foreign and Domestic Firms in Mexico'. *Journal of Management Studies* 47, no. 1: 1–26.

Newholm, Terry, Sandra Newholm, and Deirdre Shaw. 2015. 'A History for Consumption Ethics'. *Business History* 57, no. 2: 290–310.

Ng, T. W. H., K. C. Yam, and H. Aguinis. 2019. 'Employee Perceptions of Corporate Social Responsibility: Effects on Pride, Embeddedness, and Turnover'. *Personnel Psychology* 72: 107–37.

Nguyen, Phuong-Anh, Ambrus Kecskés, and Sattar Mansi, 2020. 'Does Corporate Social Responsibility Create Shareholder Value? The Importance of Long-term Investors'. *Journal of Banking & Finance* 112: 105217, ISSN 0378-4266. https://doi.org/10.1016/j.jbankfin.2017.09.013.

Nielsen, Kristina Praestbro, and Rikke Winther Noergaard. 2011. 'CSR and Mainstream Investing: A New Match?—An Analysis of the Existing ESG Integration Methods in Theory and Practice and the Way Forward'. *Journal of Sustainable Finance & Investment* 1, no. 3–4: 209–21.

Öge, Kerem. 2016. 'To Disclose or Not to Disclose: How Global Competition for Foreign Direct Investment Influences Transparency Reforms in Extractive Industries'. *Energy Policy* 98: 133–41.

Oikonomou, Ioannis, Chao Yin, and Lei Zhao. 2019. 'Investment Horizon and Corporate Social Performance: The Virtuous Circle of Long-term Institutional Ownership and Responsible Firm Conduct'. *The European Journal of Finance* 26, no. 1: 14–40.

Olson, Mancur. 1965. *The Logic of Collective Action: Public Goods and the Theory of Groups.* Cambridge, MA: Harvard University Press.

Oppong, Nelson, and Nathan Andrews. 2020. 'Extractive Industries Transparency Initiative and the Politics of Institutional Innovation in Ghana's Oil Industry'. *The Extractive Industries and Society* 7, no. 4: 1238–45.

Ortas, Eduardo, Igor Álavarez, and Ainhoa Garayar. 2015. 'The Environmental, Social, Governance, and Financial Performance Effects on Companies that Adopt the United Nations Global Compact'. *Sustainability* 7: 1932–56.

Parsa, Sepideh, Ian Roper, Michael Muller-Camen, and Eva Szigetvari. 2018. 'Have Labor Practices and Human Rights Disclosures Enhanced Corporate Accountability? The Case of the GRI Framework'. *Accounting Forum* 42, no. 1: 47–64.

Perrault, Elise, and Michael A. Quinn. 2018. 'What Have Firms Been Doing? Exploring What KLD Data Report About Firms' Corporate Social Performance in the Period 2000–2010'. *Business & Society* 57, no. 5: 890–928.

Pigou, A. C. 1920. *The Economics of Welfare.* London: Macmillan.

Polanyi, Karl. 1944. *The Great Transformation: The Political and Economic Origins of Our Time*. Boston: Beacon Press.

Pomering, Alan, and Sara Dolnicar. 2009. 'Assessing the Prerequisite of Successful CSR Implementation: Are Consumers Aware of CSR Initiatives?' *Journal of Business Ethics* 85, no. 2: 285–301.

Porter, Michael E., and Mark R. Kramer. 2011. 'Creating Shared Value'. *Harvard Business Review* 89, no. 1/2: 62–77.

Pun, Ngai, Yuan Shen, Yuhu Guo, Huilin Lu, Jenny Chan, and Mark Selden. 2016. 'Apple, Foxconn, and Chinese Workers' Struggles from a Global Labor Perspective'. *Inter-Asia Cultural Studies* 17, no. 2: 166–85.

Rahman, Sahidur, and Kazi Mahmudur Rahman. 2020. 'Multi-actor Initiatives after Rana Plaza: Factory Managers' Views'. *Development and Change* 51, no. 5: 1331–59.

Rasche, Andreas, and Sandra Waddock. 2014. 'Global Sustainability Governance and the UN Global Compact: A Rejoinder to Critics'. *Journal of Business Ethics* 122: 209–16.

Refinitv. 2021. 'Environmental, Social and Governance (ESG) Scores from Refinitiv'. Feb. Found at: https://www.refinitiv.com/en/sustainable-finance/esg-scores, Accessed July 26, 2021.

Renneboog, Luc, Jenke Ter Horst, and Chendi Zhang. 2008. 'Socially Responsible Investments: Institutional Aspects, Performance, and Investor Behavior'. *Journal of Banking & Finance* 32, no. 9: 1723–42.

Richardson, Benjamin J. 2013. 'Socially Responsible Investing for Sustainability: Overcoming Its Incomplete and Conflicting Rationales'. *Transnational Environmental Law* 2, no. 21: 311–38.

Rioux, Michèle, and Christine Vaillancourt. 2020. 'Regulating Corporate Social Responsibility (CSR) for Economic and Social Development through Trade Rules'. *Journal of Developing Societies* 36, no. 3: 335–52.

Rita Sequeira, Ana, Mark P. McHenry, Angus Morrison-Saunders, Hudson Mtegha, and David Doepel. 2016. 'Is the Extractive Industry Transparency Initiative (EITI) Sufficient to Generate Transparency in Environmental Impact and Legacy Risks? The Zambian Minerals Sector'. *Journal of Cleaner Production* 129: 427–36.

Riter, Jennifer J. 2019. 'An Exploration of the Extractive Industries Transparency Initiative as a Model for Incorporating Collaborative Accountability into Collective Global Governance'. *University of Pennsylvania International Law Journal* 40, no. 4: 839–93.

Ross, Robert J. S. 2004. *Slaves to Fashion: Abuse in the New Sweatshops*. Ann Arbor: The University of Michigan Press.

Runhaar, Hens, and Helene Lafferty. 2009. 'Governing Corporate Social Responsibility: An Assessment of the Contribution of the UN Global Compact to CSR Strategies in the Telecommunication Industry'. *Journal of Business Ethics* 84: 479–95.

Sandberg, Joakim. 2013. '(Re-)interpreting Fiduciary Duty to Justify Socially Responsible Investment for Pension Funds?' *Corporate Governance* 21, no. 5: 436–46.

Sandberg, Joakim. 2011. 'Changing the World through Shareholder Activism?' *Etikki praksis. Nordic Journal of Applied Ethics* 5, no. 1: 51–78.

Sandberg, J., Juravle, C., Hedesström, T. M. *et al.* 2009. 'The Heterogeneity of Socially Responsible Investment'. *Journal of Business Ethics* 87: 519–33.

Sasse-Werhahn, L. 2019. 'The Practical Wisdom behind the GRI'. *Humanistic Management Journal* 4: 71–84.

Scanteam. 2011. *Achievements and Strategic Options: Evaluation of the Extractive Industries Transparency Initiative*. Final Report. Oslo: Scanteam.

Scherer, Andreas Georg, and Guido Palazzo. 2011. 'The New Political Role of Business in a Globalized World: A Review of a New Perspective on CSR and Its Implications for the Firm, Governance, and Democracy'. *Journal of Management Studies* 48, no. 4: 899–931.

Scholtens, Bert, and Rikka Sievänen. 2013. 'Drivers of Socially Responsible Investing: A Case Study of Four Nordic Countries'. *Journal of Business Ethics* 115, no. 3: 605–16.

Scott, W. R. 2014. *Institutions and Organizations: Ideas, Interests and Identities*, 4th ed. Thousand Oaks, CA: Sage.

Securities and Exchange Commission of the U.S. 2021. 'The Division of Examinations' Review of ESG Investing. Risk Alert: Division of Examinations'. April 9. Found at: https://www.sec.gov/sec-response-climate-and-esg-risks-and-opportunities, Accessed July 29, 2021.

Seidman, Gay W. 2007. *Beyond the Boycott: Labor Rights, Human Rights, and Transnational Activism*. NY: Russell Sage Foundation.

Servaes, Henri, and Ane Tamayo. 2013. 'The Impact of Corporate Social Responsibility on Firm Value: The Role of Customer Awareness'. *Management Science* 59, no. 5: 1045–61.

Sethi, S. P., and D. H. Schepers, 2014. 'United Nations Global Compact: The Promise–Performance Gap'. *Journal of Business Ethics* 122: 193–208.

Simpson, Cam, Akshat Rathi, and Saijel Kishan. 2021. 'The ESG Mirage: MSCI, the Largest ESG Rating Company, Doesn't Even Try to Measure the Impact of a Corporation on the World. It's All about Whether the World might Mess with the Bottom Line'. *Bloomberg Businessweek*. December 9. Found at: https://www.bloomberg.com/graphics/2021-what-is-esg-investing-msci-ratings-focus-on-corporate-bottom-line/, Accessed December 21, 2021.

Soederberg, Susanne, 2007. 'Socially Responsible Investment and the Development Agenda: Peering Behind the Progressive Veil of Non-financial Benchmarking'. *Third World Quarterly* 28, no. 7: 1219–37.

Sovacool, Benjamin K. 2020. 'Is Sunshine the Best Disinfectant? Evaluating the Global Effectiveness of the Extractive Industries Transparency Initiative (EITI)'. *The Extractive Industries and Society* 7, no. 4: 1451–71.

Sovacool, Benjamin K., and Nathan Andrews. 2015. 'Does Transparency Matter? Evaluating the Governance Impacts of the Extractive Industries Transparency Initiative (EITI) in Azerbaijan and Liberia'. *Resources Policy* 45: 183–92.

Stiglitz, Joseph E., and Michael Rothschild. 1976. 'Equilibrium in Competitive Insurance Markets: An Essay on the Economics of Imperfect Information'. *The Quarterly Journal of Economics* 90, no. 4: 629–49.

Stobierski, Tim. 2021. '15 Eye-Opening Corporate Social Responsibility Statistics'. *Harvard Business School Online*. Found at: https://online.hbs.edu/blog/post/corporate-social-responsibility-statistics, Accessed December 2, 2021.

Surroca, Jordi, Josep A. Tribó, and Sandra Waddock. 2010. 'Corporate Responsibility and Financial Performance: The Role of Intangible Resources'. *Strategic Management* 31, no. 5: 463–90.

SustainAbility. 2020.' Investor Survey and Interview Results'. ERM Group.

Swyngedouw, Eric. 2005. 'Governance Innovation and the Citizen: The Janus Face of Governance-beyond-the-State'. *Urban Studies* 42, no. 11: 1991–2006.

Tang, Dragon Yongjun, Jiali Yan, and Chelsea Yaqiong Yao. 2021. 'The Determinants of ESG Ratings: Rater Ownership Matters'. Working Paper. July 18. Found at SSRN: http://dx.doi.org/10.2139/ssrn.3889395, Accessed July 27, 2021.

Tarabashkina, L., O. Tarabashkina, P. Quester, and G. N. Soutar. 2020. 'Does Corporate Social Responsibility Improve Brands' Responsible and Active Personality Dimensions? An Experimental Investigation'. *Journal of Product & Brand Management* 30, no. 7: 1016–32.

Tashman, P., V. Marano, and T. Kostova. 2019. 'Walking the Walk or Talking the Talk? Corporate Social Responsibility Decoupling in Emerging Market Multinationals'. *Journal of Business Ethics* 50: 153–71. https://doi.org/10.1057/s41267-018-0171-7.

Trebilcock, Anne. 2020. 'The Rana Plaza Disaster Seven Years on: Transnational Experiments and Perhaps a New Treaty?' *International Labor Review* 159, no. 4: 545–68.

Trinks, Pieter Jan, and Bert Scholtens. 2017. 'The Opportunity Cost of Negative Screening in Socially Responsible Investing'. *Journal of Business Ethics* 140: 193–208.

United Nations Global Compact. '2020 Annual Management Report'. Found at: https://www.unglobalcompact.org/about/finances, Accessed June 17, 2021.

————. 2015. 'Integrity Measures Policy'. Found at: https://www.unglobalcompact.org/about/integrity-measures, Accessed June 17, 2021.

Urkidi, Leire. 2010. 'A Global Environmental Movement against Gold Mining: Pascua–Lama in Chile'. *Ecological Economics* 70, no. 2: 219–27.

Urkidi, Leire, and Mariana Walter. 2011. 'Dimensions of Environmental Justice in Anti-gold Mining Movements in Latin America'. *Geoforum* 42, no. 6: 683–95.

van Marrewijk, Marcel. 2003. 'Concepts and Definitions of CSR and Corporate Sustainability: Between Agency and Communion'. *Journal of Business Ethics* 44, no. 2/3: 95–105.

Varkey Foundation. 2016. *Business Backs Education: Creating a Baseline for Corporate CSR Spend on Global Education Initiatives*. London: Varkey Foundation.

Vernon, Raymond. 1971. *Sovereignty at Bay: The Multinational Spread of U.S. Enterprises*. NY: Basic Books.

Vijge, Marjanneke J. 2018. 'The (Dis)empowering Effects of Transparency Beyond Information Disclosure: The Extractive Industries Transparency Initiative in Myanmar'. *Global Environmental Politics* 18, no. 1: 13–32.

Vogel, David. 2010. 'The Private Regulation of Global Corporate Conduct: Achievements and Limitations'. *Business & Society* 49, no. 10: 68–87.

Waddock, S. A., and Graves, S. B. 1997. 'The Corporate Social Performance–Financial Performance Link'. *Strategic Management Journal* 18: 303–19.

Wagemans, Frank A. J., C. S. A. (Kris) van Koppen, and Arthur P. J. Mol. 2013. 'The Effectiveness of Socially Responsible Investment: A Review'. *Journal of Integrative Environmental Sciences* 10, no. 3–4: 235–52.

Waldman, D., M. Sully de Luque, and N. Washburn, *et al.* 2006. 'Cultural and Leadership Predictors of Corporate Social Responsibility Values of Top Management: A GLOBE Study of 15 Countries'. *Journal of Business Ethics* 37: 823.

Walker, Owen, and Camilla Hodgson. 2021. ' "Greenwashing": Do the Maths on Mark Carney's US$130-trillion Net Zero Pledge Stack up?" *Financial Times*. November 9. Found at: https://financialpost.com/commodities/energy/greenwashing-do-the-maths-on-mark-carneys-us130-trillion-net-zero-pledge-stack-up, Accessed December 21, 2021.

Whitehouse, Lisa. 2006. 'Corporate Social Responsibility: Views from the Frontline'. *Journal of Business Ethics* 63: 279–96.

Wood, Donna J. 1991. 'Corporate Social Performance Revisited'. *Academy of Management Review* 16, no. 4: 691–718.

Yuan, Y., G. Tian, L. Lu, *et al.* 2019. 'CEO Ability and Corporate Social Responsibility'. *Journal of Business Ethics* 157: 391–411.

Zalik, Anna, and Isaac 'Asume' Osuoka. 2020. 'Beyond Transparency: A Consideration of Extraction's Full Costs'. *The Extractive Industries and Society* 7, no. 3: 781–85.

Appendix A

ALLEGATIONS OF SERIOUS HUMAN RIGHTS VIOLATIONS RELATED TO MULTINATIONAL COMPANIES IN MINING, APPAREL, AND ELECTRONICS SECTORS

The following sections offer the raw data for the most serious allegations of company killings or deaths, based on multiple sources.

Mining

We examined conflicts reported by the Environmental Justice Atlas (EJAtlas) (https://ejatlas.org/, accessed July 20, 2021). The EJAtlas reports on global conflicts around resource extraction and is backed by the European Union. There is a total dataset of 3,490 global conflicts reported. We used the following filters to reduce the cases to the most egregious and conflictual ones around corporate behavior: mineral ores and building materials extraction (sector filter); high intensity (widespread, mass mobilization, violence, arrests, etc. […]); corruption; deaths, assassinations, murders, violent targeting of activists; and repression. This yielded twenty-six cases reported on the EJAtlas. The conflicts noted there were verified again on OCMAL, the Latin American Observatory for Mining Conflicts (https://www.ocmal. org/, accessed July 20, 2021). They indicate that the following companies had ongoing issues with community conflict: Barrick Gold, Newmont Mining, Goldcorp, and Rio Tinto.

Case	Country	Company	Year	Investment level ($)	Mineral	Verified on OCMAL	Comments
Pascua Lama	Chile	Barrick Gold Corp. (Canada)	2001	1.5 billion	Gold	Yes	Proximity to glaciers sparks protests, lawsuit and fines; suspended since 2013; shutdown in 2018
Pierina, Jangas	Peru	Barrick Gold Corp.(Canada)	2002	n/a	Gold	Yes	Protests based on lack of local economic development, environmental concerns; police allegedly killed protestors in 2006/2012
La Zanja	Peru	Newmont Mining Corp. (US); Compania Minera Buenaventura (Peru)	2004–13	50 million	Silver, gold	Yes	Proposed project; environmental protests in 2004, 2007, 2008; mining suspended in region from 2013
Conga	Peru	Newmont Mining Corp. (US); Minera Yanacocha SRL (Peru); Minas Buenaventura (Peru); Corporacion Financiera Internacional (Peru); Sumitomo Corp. (Japan)	2010–13	4.5 billion	Gold, silver, copper	Yes	Environmental protests from 2011; suspended since 2013
Marlin	Guatemala	Goldcorp (Can.), Glamis Gold (Can.), Montana Exploradora de Guatemala	2005	800 million	Silver, gold	Yes	Project suspended in 2017 after local and global protests

Note: Filters: category: mineral ore exploration; intensity: high; outcome: corruption; deaths, assassinations, and murders; violent targeting of activists; and repression.

Sources: https://ejatlas.org/ and https://mapa.conflictosmineros.net/ocmal_db-v2/conflicto/view/12, both accessed July 20, 2021.

Company	HQ Country	Country of Violations	Year	Comments
MMG	Australia	Peru, Las Bambas mine	2018	Protests leading to violence
Rio Tinto	Australia	Mozambique, Papua New Guinea, Indonesia	2017, 2013, 2014	Source: HRWatch; forcible relocation of farmers; HR abuses; mine fatality
OceanaGold	Australia	Philippines, El Sal.	2016, 2018	HR+ environmental issues; led to OG lawsuit against El Sal Govt.
Vale-BSGR	Brazil	Guinea	2018	Lawsuit over alleged violence by defense and company security forces against villagers
Vale/BHP Billiton	Brazil/ Australia	Brazil	2015–8	Major tailings dam collapse, plenty of coverage
Fortuna Silver Mines	Canada	Mexico	2012–3; 2018	Violence and water contamination
Tahoe Resources	Canada	Guatemala	2010–17	Major protests and lawsuit
Goldcorp	Canada	Guatemala	2010–17	Marlin Mine, lawsuit in Canada
Barrick	Canada	Tanzania/ Papua New Guinea	2010–18	Environmental protests over water rights
HudBay Minerals	Canada	Guatemala	2010–17	Security chief killed and paralyzed indigenous leader
NevSun Resources	Canada	Eritrea	2016	Forced labor allegation
B2Gold	Canada	Nicaragua	2015	El Limon mine, death at a
Anvil Mining	Canada (Chinese own %)	DRCongo	2010–15	protest 2004 armed attack led to 2017 $4.36 million award to DR Congo victims; mining company provided transport to Congolese armed forces who allegedly killed protestors (and other HR violations)
St. Augustine	Singapore	Philippines	2018	Opposition to mine leader Audo Quillo shot in 2018 by unidentified assailants

(Continued)

Company	HQ Country	Country of Violations	Year	Comments
Harmony Gold	South Africa	South Africa	2012–18	Workers trapped in fire, killings 2012 killing of 34
Lonmin	South Africa	South Africa	2012–18	striking miners by S. Afr. Police in Marikana; lawsuit
Anglo American	South Africa	South Africa	2013–18	Silicosis and TB of miners lawsuit
AngloGold Ashanti	South Africa	South Africa	2013–18	Silicosis and TB of miners lawsuit
Gold Fields	South Africa	South Africa	2013–18	Silicosis and TB of miners lawsuit
Glencore	Switzerland	Peru, Philippines, DRC	2015, 2014, 2012–14	DRC—including environmental impacts
Vedanta Resources	UK	India	2018–19	5,000 tribal leaders protested in March 2019; 2 were killed by Odisha Industrial Security Force; killings of 14 in May 2018 by Thoothikudi police; Copper smelter closed in 2018
Drummond Mining	US	Colombia	2011–16	Used paramilitaries to repress workers negligence
Newmont	US	Ghana	2018	for death of workers in Ahafo

Note: Filter: "killings" or "death" for the mining sector; multiple stories.

Source: BHRR, accessed July 22, 2021.

Clothing and Footwear

BHRR Source		Deaths or Killings
Company	HQ Country	Countries of Alleged Violations & Years
Asics	Japan	Cambodia (2013), factory collapse kills 2 (also featured in WSJ)
H&M	Sweden	Cambodia (2013), factory collapse kills 2 (also featured in WSJ)
Loblaw	Canada	Bangladesh (2013–17), Rana Plaza factory blg. Collapse
Canadian Tire	Canada	Bangladesh (2013–17), Rana Plaza factory blg. Collapse
Primark	Irish	Bangladesh (2013–17), Rana Plaza factory blg. Collapse
JC Penney	US	Bangladesh (2013–17), Rana Plaza factory blg. Collapse
WalMart	US	Bangladesh (2013–17), Rana Plaza factory blg. Collapse
Zara	Spain	Bangladesh (2013–17), Rana Plaza factory blg. Collapse
Mango	Spain	Bangladesh (2013–17), Rana Plaza factory blg. Collapse
Gucci	Italy	Bangladesh (2013–17), Rana Plaza factory blg. Collapse
Versace	Italy	Bangladesh (2013–17), Rana Plaza factory blg. Collapse
Nike	US	Uzbekistan (2013); 18-year-old Navruz Muyzinov died after being beaten by police for leaving cotton field w/o meeting quoto
Uniqlo	Japan	China (2015); alleged death from electrocution; excessive working hours; lack of worker safety

https://www.business-humanrights.org/en/, accessed July 22, 2021; search for "killings" or "deaths".

HRW Source		Any Human Rights Violations
H&M	Sweden	Cambodia (2015), labor rights abuses
Loblaw	Canada	Cambodia (2015), labor rights abuses
Marks and Spencer	UK	Cambodia (2015), labor rights abuses
The Gap	US	Cambodia (2015), labor rights abuses

www.hrw.org, accessed July 21, 2021.

WRC Source		Human Rights Violations
Adidas	Germany	Multiple sites (2002–present)
New Balance	US	Thailand (2009); Cambodia (2017); China (2021)
Nike	US	Multiple sites (2006–present)
Reebok	Germany	Multiple sites (2006–9); subsidiary of Adidas from 2005
Asics	Japan	China (2014)
The Gap	US	Multiple sites (2005–present)
Uniqlo	Japan	Indonesia (2015)
JC Penney	US	India (2010); Indonesia (2011); Nicaragua (2013)
WalMart	US	India (2010); Bang. (2012); Nic. (2013); Haiti (2013); El Sal. (2013, 2015, 2019): Cambod. (2014); Ethiopia (2018)

https://www.workersrights.org/our-work/factory-investigations/, accessed July 21, 2021.

Electronics

BHRR Website			
Company	HQ	Place of Alleged Violation and Years	Comment
Apple	US	China (2010–16)	Foxconn & Biel Crystal subcontractors (worker suicides)
Foxconn	Taiwan	China (2010–16)	Worker suicides
Microsoft	US	China (2010–15)	Links to Foxconn subcontractors
Dell	US	China (2010–15)	Links to Foxconn subcontractors
Nintendo	Japan	China (2010–15)	Links to Foxconn subcontractors
HP	US	China (2010–15)	Links to Foxconn subcontractors
Sony	Japan	China (2010–15)	Links to Foxconn subcontractors
Samsung	South Korea	South Korea (2013–17)	Allegations of cancer at factories

https://www.business-humanrights.org/en/, accessed July 22, 2021.

Good Electronics Website			
Apple	US	China (2010, 2011, 2013)	links to Foxconn subcontractors; child worker dies on production line in 2013
Foxconn	Taiwan	China (2010, 2011, 2013), Brazil (2017)	Worker suicides
Samsung	South Korea	S. Korea; Brazil (2017); Vietnam (2018)	Death from cancer; methanol poisoning by subcontractors in 2017 in Brazil; exposure to toxic chemicals
Philips	Netherlands	Brazil (2015)	Workers in Brazil contaminated with mercury
LG	South Korea	Brazil (2017)	Methanol poisoning by subcontractors in 2017

https://goodelectronics.org/, accessed July 21, 2021; "death".

Other Allegations Based on Amnesty International Reports

In order to examine events of the most egregious human rights abuses, we also checked the Amnesty International website (https://www.amnesty.org, accessed July 21, 2021). Amnesty is considered one of the leading NGOs monitoring human rights around the world and uses a variety of primary research methods. Using their search engine, we examined all reports related to "business and human rights" and "corporate accountability" for the years 2016–2017. We highlighted the well-known multinational companies that came up in regard to human rights abuse allegations (report date in quotes). Shell's activities in Nigeria around human rights abuses in the Niger Delta region were the subject of a report (November 28, 2017 and June 29, 2017). A report on child labor and environmental hazards in the cobalt industry gave failing grades to Renault; ZTE Corp. Vodafone Group; Microsoft Corp; Lenovo Group; and Huawei Technologies (November 15, 2017). Another report noted serious labor exploitation and abuse in Indonesia by Wilmar International, the world's largest processor of palm oil, which is purchased by companies such as AFAMSA; Archer Daniels Midland (ADM); Colgate-Palmolive; Elevance Renewable Sciences; The Kellogg Company; Nestlé; Reckitt Benckiser; Unilever; and Procter & Gamble (November 30, 2016). The (August 15, 2016) report cites deaths at the Marikana mine run by the company Lonmin, a UK mining company that was acquired by Sibanye-Stillwater, a South African company. It is also worth mentioning the 2014 Frontline and ProPublica investigations of the alleged support by Firestone of Liberian warlord Charles Taylor.

INDEX

Abbott, Kenneth W. and Snidal, Duncan,
    mixed regime theory 31, 33
Accountability, definitions of 9
Anti-capitalism 4–5
Apparel
    allegations 85, 92–93
    case study 84–85
    human rights violations
Apparel Industry Partnership 19
Apple 25, 111, see also Foxconn
Auditing
    and conflicts of interest 106–107
    deficiencies 33–35, 79–81, 101

Bloomberg, Michael 54–55, 101
    Bloomberg rating agency 52, 56,
        65, 88, 97
Boiral, Olivier 35, 42, 56–57
"Boomerang effect" (of human rights
    violations reporting) 10
Brands 16, 26
British Petroleum 1, 20
Business case for CSR 22–24
Business & Human Rights Resource
    (BHRR) 82, 84

CalPERS (California Public Employees'
    Retirement System)
    pension fund 53, 67–69
Carney, Mark 2
Carroll, Archie B. 20–21, 28
Civil society
    and EITI 43–44, 48
    lack of consideration of 110
    and mining 49, 69–70, 98, 102–104, 106
    participation in mixed regimes 41

Climate change 18, 54–55, 59,
    see also Sustainability Accounting
    Standards Board, and
    Non-Financial Reporting Directive
Collective action theory 8–9, 29
    club goods 10, 30
    and ESG 101–103
Consumer attitudes towards CSR
    2–3, 24–25, 27
Corporate culture, see Management Values
Corporate Social Responsibility (CSR)
    expenditures on 2
    general definition 1, 19
    global CSR regimes 5
    historical roots 15, 19
    links to return on investment 22–24
    outcomes 73, 107
    reasons for 2–3, 15, 20–21
    and "triple bottom line", 3
Corruption (of governments) 45,
    see also Governance Paradox
    protests against 48

Deregulation, see Neoliberalism
Dow Jones Sustainability Index (DJSI) 23

EITI (Extractive Industries Transparency
    Initiative) 33, 42–49
    and accountability 46
    board composition 43
    and enforcement 44–45
    impact 46
Electronics
    case study 85
    human rights violations allegations
        85, 94–95

Employee attitudes towards CSR 3
ESG (Environment, Social and
    Governance) accountability for 59
  controversies indicators 86–88
  deficiencies 65–67, 96, 99–100
  definition, indicators 18, 101–102
  and fiduciary responsibility 56
  firm characteristics and 23
  methodologies 60, 65–66
  lack of standards 56–57, 99–100
  outcomes 75–78, 80, 104
  ratings agencies 60–65
  use by money managers 56–58
  and SRI 51
Ethical Trading Initiative (ETI) 19, 34
European Trading System (ETS) 6
European Union (EU)
  harmonization efforts with the US
      53, 100
  regulations around CSR/SRI
      5–6, 54–56
Externalities 7–8

Factiva 81–82, 86
Fair Labor Association (FLA) 19, 78
Fair trade 27
Fiduciary/Shareholder responsibility
    19, 56–57, 97–98, 100
Financial Stability Board 54–55
"Financialization" (rise of finance) 16
Forest Stewardship Council 30
Foxconn, worker suicides 77–78
Friedman, Milton 1, 16, 19
FTSE4 Good Sustainability Index 62–63

Global Compact (United Nations)
    18, 32, 36–39
  board composition 36
  impact 37–39, 73
Global Governance 9
Global Reporting Initiative (GRI)
    39–42, 56–57
  and accountability 41–42
  board composition 40
Governance 21
"Governance Paradox" (failure to build
    local capacity) 77, 104–105, 110

Institutional theory 20, 26
International Labor Organization 107
International Organizations 9, 11,
    27, 30, 32–33, 38, 49–50, 62,
    see also Mixed Regimes
Isomorphism (corporate mimetic
    behavior) 25–26

KLD rating agency, see MSCI

Labor Unions 15, 17, 110
Legal cases around CSR and SRI 53

Management values and 22, 26, 28
Methodology (of this study) 73–74,
    81–82, 88, 92
Mining 32–33, see also Pascua
    Lama and Vale
  and conflicts 69–70, 74
  and EITI 33, 35, 45, 47–49
  and ESG ratings 61
  and GRI 42
  human rights violations allegations
      83, 89–91
  study of ESG reporting 82–84, 89
Mixed Regimes 31–35
  definition 32
  governance of 48, see also Global
      Compact, Global Reporting
      Initiative, and Extractive
      Industries Initiative
MSCI
  comparison to Refinitiv ratings 94
  ESG rating agency 23, 61–62, 70–71
  and Global Compact 39–40
MSIntegrity, report on mixed regimes
    34–35, 45
Multi-stakeholder Initiatives (MSIs),
    see Mixed Regimes

Neoliberalism 20
NGOs (non-governmental organizations)
    10, 17
  and accountability 49–50, 69, 80–81,
      101, 105, 109–110
  and mixed regimes 32–33
Nike 12, 19, 25, 34
Non-financial Reporting Directive 55

Pascua Lama (case study) 74–76, 86–88
Patagonia Clothing 22, 26
Pension funds 10, 18
Polanyi 4, 15
Porter, Michael 3
Power of corporations 4–5, 106–107
Principles for Responsible Investment
    (PRI) 18, 53–54
Privatization, see Neoliberalism

Rana Plaza (factory disaster) 78–81,
    105, 108–109
Reasons/incentives for CSR 3
Refinitiv, see Thomson-Reuters
Regime theory 9, 30–32
Regulation 17
Reporting, elements of a good system
    11–12
Return on Investment, see Business
    case for CSR
RIT (Regulator, Intermediary,
    and Target) theory,
    see Abbot and Snidal

SAI (Social Accountability
    International) 30
Screening 57–58, 105
    by CalPERS 68–69
Securities and Exchange Commission
    (US Government)
    and ESG 59
Shareholder activism 10, 26–28
Shareholder responsibility, see Fiduciary
    Responsibility
Social license/stakeholder view of CSR 3
Social movements 6–7, 17
Socially responsible investment
    amounts 18, 51–52

definition 18
EU vs. US regulations 5–6
information systems around 18–19
limitations of methodology 65–67
methodology 60–61
outcomes 73, 100, 107
power of 111
quality of information for 56–58
reasons for 5, 51
and return on investment 58–59
Soft law 30
Sustainability Accounting Standards
    Board (SASB) 55, 97
Sustainability Ratings Agencies (SRA) 56
Sustainalytics, rating agency 63

Task Force for Climate-Related
    Disclosures 54
Thomson Reuters 82
Thomson-Reuters Refinitiv,
    ESG rating agency 64–65
TIAA-CREF 53
Transactions costs 8–9
Transparency 9

Unions 33, 50–51, 53, 110
    historical importance of in the West 15, 17
    labor repression of 79
United Nations, see Global Compact
Universal Owner theory 52–53

Vale Mariana Tailings Dam Disaster
    76–77
Varieties of capitalism 5
Vigeo-Ethical Investor Research Service
    (EIRIS) 63–64

Walmart 92, 94

www.ingramcontent.com/pod-product-compliance
Lightning Source LLC
Chambersburg PA
CBHW020614270326
41927CB00005B/334